BAPTISTS WHO SHAPED A NATION

O. K. AND MARJORIE ARMSTRONG

BROADMAN PRESS
Nashville, Ten

© Copyright 1975 • Broadman Press
ISBN: 0-8054-6517-0 (paperback)
4265-17 (paperback)
4288-03 (BRP)

Library of Congress Catalog Card Number: 74-27925
Dewey Decimal Classification: 286.09
Printed in the United States of America

unyielding.' In their early days on these shores the Baptists
suffered opposition, endured injustice, and underwent widespread persecution. Yet, far from being subdued or overcome,
they thrived to become far and away the largest Protestant
body. And they have been unyielding in their original and
peculiar doctrines. At no time have they sought to curry
public favor or to modify their tenets for the sake of general
acceptance. . . .

"Baptist influence has operated on both the personal and
social levels in America. In the matter of shared belief there
has been consistency. Insistence upon immersion as the
proper form of baptism, opposition to infant baptism, a
survival of medieval ritualism, belief in the autonomy of
every one of the 97,000 local churches—these are tenets
on which Baptists unite in mind. The presence of thirty
identifiable groupings in the United States testifies to the
range of variety within the denomination and to the allow-
ance for the intense individuality of opinion within the
faith—to the right of Baptists to worship as they please.

"The defense and extension of this right has been from
the first a characteristic activity of the Baptists. They are
allied with the cause of religious liberty and it is in this
cause that they have shown demonstrable influence on
American political history. . . . Groups who dissented from
the established faith had to pay the price of dissent in the
form of taxes to support the authorized church.

"Those who cried out loudest against this taxing practice
were the Baptists. When they spoke of religious liberty they
were not talking merely about an abstract principle. They
were talking about the specific rights of individual believers
and of organized church bodies. And when the Baptists
agitated successfully to include provisions for religious liberty in the Bill of Rights added to the Constitution they

TO BEGIN WITH

When a major publishing company in New York launched a series of books in the 1960's on "Religion in America" and gave us the opportunity to write the book on the Baptists, we spent two years refreshing our memories on our own people and reading history books.

In 1967, our 400-page volume appeared under the title *The Indomitable Baptists,* "A Narrative of Their Role in Shaping American History." We were gratified at the sale of this book.

We were humbly grateful when Broadman Press asked that six of the first chapters of our book be allowed to appear in a volume for the Broadman Readers Plan. We are pleased with this opportunity to perpetuate the usefulness of the larger book.

The editor of the "Religion in America" series, Charles W. Ferguson, a Methodist layman, stated the reason for the choice of the original title:

"If it were possible to sum up in a word the temper and spirit of a religious group as diverse and numerous as the Baptists, the word 'indomitable' would do it; 'that cannot be overcome or subdued by labors, difficulties, or opposition;

CONTENTS

To Begin With   vii

1. JOHN LELAND
    The Baptist Who Made a Political Deal
    with James Madison   9

2. ROGER WILLIAMS
    The Baptist Who Befriended Persons
    "Distressed of Conscience"   31

3. JOHN CLARKE
    The Baptist Who Wrested a Charter
    of Freedom from King Charles   53

4. WILLIAM SCREVEN
    The Baptist Who Planted a Free Church
    in Warm, Rich Soil   69

5. ISAAC BACKUS
    The Baptist Who Lobbied
    for Religious Freedom Against John Adams   82

6. SUNDRY PATRIOTS
    The Baptists Who Proclaimed
    Freedom of Soul, Southward and Westward   100

And Finally . . .
    From the Past to the Future   119

Notes   121

were in harmony with their own history as well as their faith."

We are glad that this new book, which is a reprint of so much of the earlier book, can appear at a time when the nation is celebrating its 200th birthday. We hope it will be widely read and that it will stimulate a new appreciation of how Baptists helped to bring this nation to maturity.

O. K. Armstrong
Marjorie M. Armstrong

"The Highlands"
Republic, Missouri 65738

1

JOHN LELAND
The Baptist Who Made a Political Deal
with James Madison

Into the Williams Meeting House in Goochland County, Virginia, on the bright morning of March 7, 1788, strode about a score of the gentlemen of the Virginia Baptist General Committee. The majority were ministers, the others active laymen. They had ridden in from various parts of the state, but most of them lived in Goochland, Orange, and Culpeper counties where Baptist churches were strongest and Baptist influence most powerful.

Leader of these devout men was John Leland, an earnest and vigorous preacher and writer, who lived on a spacious farm near Orange on the Fredericksburg road. Leland was born at Grafton, Massachusetts, in May, 1754, and had migrated to Virginia in 1776 for the principal reason that he felt impelled to combat the persecutions of Baptists and other nonconformists in the Old Dominion. He was now recognized as the eloquent spokesman for Baptists in the state, pleading the cause of religious liberty and complete separation of church and government.

John Leland counted Thomas Jefferson, Patrick Henry, and James Madison his personal friends. Each of these Virginia politicians had sought and accepted his advice through the years. When John Leland spoke, men of all faiths and of all callings listened attentively.

Leland had issued the call for this meeting of the Baptist General Committee to consider a matter of great importance: Should the Baptists of Virginia support the ratification by the General Assembly of the new federal constitution?

The question had been raised by the Baptists, but not because they opposed the plan for a federal union. Their leaders and members generally were not antagonistic to a higher sovereignty, which the new constitution proposed. The question had been raised because of concern over an apparent lack of guarantees for complete religious liberty in the new basic law.

In the main, citizens of all faiths in Virginia were satisfied with the proposed constitution. Baptists had shared the pride of Episcopalians, Congregationalists, Quakers, Methodists, and others that the commonwealth's noblest son, George Washington, had presided over the Constitutional Convention in Philadelphia. Truly, this man who had been first in war and who had led the Continental Army to victory was proving himself to be first in peace. That Washington would be named the first President when the Union was formed was taken for granted.

There had been anxiety over the slow progress of the convention during the first weeks of that historic session. As the information from Philadelphia trickled back in summaries of the proceedings in the weekly newspapers, many feared that differences of opinion would prevent any union being formed. The delegates faced such big questions as what sort of legislature should be established, whether the small states could trust the large ones in a federated republic, and how to divide the powers so that no man or set of men could ever seize control of the government.

There was general satisfaction when it was announced that aging Benjamin Franklin had suggested that since the convention had reached no major agreement in six weeks the members should begin the sessions with prayer "to seek the guidance of Divine Power." There was a saying among Baptists: "Even if Old Ben Franklin is not a Baptist, he is acting like one!"

The facts that the proceedings moved along after that with greater speed and less dissension, that the difficulty of forming a union out of big and little states was settled by a compromise that allowed each state two senators, and that a division of powers was agreed to that seemed to protect the people with suitable checks and balances, were taken as an indication of divine leadership.

"Where Are the Guarantees?"

There was additional satisfaction throughout the Old Dominion that her delegates had supported the wording in Article VI which read: ". . . but no religious test shall ever be required as a qualification to any office of public trust under the United States." That provision effectively outlawed any chance that the federal government could make religious beliefs or nonbeliefs a qualification for office, a principle that Baptists everywhere had traditionally held to.

So the new constitution had evoked favorable reactions all over the commonwealth. Could anyone raise any doubts about a constitution formed under the leadership of such great minds as Virginia's own George Washington and James Madison, as Benjamin Franklin and Samuel Adams?

The Reverend John Leland had such doubts, and he raised them with his well-known vigor. "Where are the guarantees of complete religious liberty?" he asked. "Where is the protection for the individual to believe or not to believe, to worship or not to worship, to be free to support his church or any religious cause, and free also from all compulsion of the government to support some church? Remember—we stand for religious liberty!"

On the great Virginia plantations of the Tidewater, in all the towns from the coast to the mountains, among religious leaders of all denominations and kinds, Leland's statements were repeated and debated.

"The prohibition against any religious qualification for holding office is protection enough!" some argued. "Would any Congress or executive dare to abridge religious liberty with the principle of no religious test for office so clearly stated?"

In his many discussions on the subject during the months that followed the announcement of the new constitution, John Leland persisted in his theory that some future President or Congress just *might* seek to favor some church or some religious belief over another or might even prohibit by law or regulation the free exercise of conscience and worship. In many communities over the broad expanse of Virginia, with a persistence that marked his whole life, he won religious leaders to his view.

Now in the Williams meeting Leland was determined to put the entire Virginia fellowship on record. The gentlemen who gathered at the Meeting House on that March morning in 1788 needed no further arguments. Their minds were made up. They agreed upon a statement that included these words:

"We the Virginia Baptist General Committee unanimously hold that the new federal constitution, proposed to the States for their ratification, does not make sufficient provision for the secure enjoyment of religious liberty; and therefore it should be amended to make such provision."

Not a man at that gathering could possibly have imagined how far and wide would spread the ripples caused by their tossing this pebble of religious principle into the lake of national politics. For the Baptist spokesmen did more than call for an amendment to the constitution. One of those present, Colonel Charles Barbour, had announced as a candidate for delegate to the state convention called to consider ratification of the new federal constitution. Now he declared that he would withdraw if Leland himself would enter the race to represent Orange County. The influential former officer in the War for Independence told the Baptist leader:

"Announce for delegate! In that way you will be able to block the ratification of the constitution. Without Virginia the constitution will never be accepted. A new convention will be forced to permit a clear statement guaranteeing religious freedom!"

Colonel Barbour's proposal was heartily seconded by several of those present. At first Leland strongly demurred. He reminded his colleagues that James Madison, the very man honored as the father of the Constitution because of his work and influence at Philadelphia in shaping the document, had announced for delegate to the Convention on Ratification. Leland did not want to be pitted against his friend Mr. Madison.

"But without Baptist support Mr. Madison can never be elected from Orange!" Colonel Barbour insisted.

The best the men could get out of John Leland was a promise to consider the matter and do what his conscience might dictate.

Following the dictates of his conscience was a firm and constant practice of the Rev. John Leland. It was his conscience that called him into the ministry and that sent him to champion religious liberty in Virginia. He had not been born of the cloth. His father was a Massachusetts farmer. John was apprenticed to a shoemaker in Hopkinton, and he became an expert cobbler.

A young belle of the community, Sallie Devine, brought in her shoes to be mended and fell in love with the handsome mender. Sallie's parents were devout Baptists and regularly attended the services at the Hopkinton Baptist meeting house. Sallie talked John into hearing Preacher Everett Jones, a man who had been severely whipped as punishment for preaching without the permission of the Massachusetts authorities. In time John professed religion, was baptized, and took up preaching himself.

Soon after he and Sallie Devine were married, they pulled up stakes for the long journey to Virginia. Self-educated by constant reading, a man of tremendous energy, Leland found and established churches in which to preach. He became known and respected as the outstanding minister of his faith in the Old Dominion.

From the Goochland County meeting of the Baptist General Committee, John Leland rode back to his home under the great oaks on the Fredericksburg road, a deeply troubled man. Here was the opportunity of a lifetime to strike the greatest possible blow for religious freedom—not for Virginia alone, but for all future citizens of the new Union of states. While he did not want to run against the very popular Mr. Madison, Leland had decided to do everything within reason and honor to defeat the ratification of the new constitution unless it included a guarantee of full religious liberty with separation of church and state.

During the days of soul-searching that followed, Preacher John Leland must have reflected many times on the reasons for his unshakable determination in the matter. He must have reviewed the persecutions of his own Baptist dissenters, and highly resolved to do all in his power to see that such unjust treatment could never again blot the record of human freedom in America. He had come to Virginia for that purpose, and his battle had been won. He knew that now was the time to lay the foundation of full religious freedom in the basic law of the new nation.

From the earliest Jamestown settlements, Virginia had been the cradle of Anglican faith in America. By the mid-eighteenth century a few struggling Baptist churches had been established in the colony. Their numbers soon grew to proportions that alarmed and distressed the clergy and leaders of the Episcopal Church, recognized by law and custom as the establishment for religion. The Baptists made themselves exceedingly unpopular with the authorities, nearly all of whom were of the establishment, by their doctrinal beliefs and practices. They refused to have their babies baptized on the ground that church membership should be entirely a voluntary matter and should follow regeneration by faith. They cried out against what they called wickedness in high places, not sparing members of the establishment if they suspected them of such things as dancing, card playing, or usury. They energetically prose-lyted for converts wherever they could find them—especially among the poorer classes of people. All in all, the Baptists refused to observe the decorum considered proper for members of a tolerated sect.

The Dissenters of Virginia

By 1760 a bitter battle was underway, launched by Epis-copal clergy and representatives of the Crown, to persecute and if possible exterminate these troublesome dissenters. There followed hundreds of arrests and imprisonments of ministers of the Baptists, Quakers, and other nonconformist groups who refused to abide by the regulations for licensing of religious bodies and payment of taxes for support of the established church.

There were laws and ordinances in Virginia, as in all the colonial states, against disturbances of the peace and vagrancy. The latter offense included "strolling," a charge which could be stretched to cover walking along without any set destination or any immediate gainful activity. These offenses were alleged in most of the charges lodged against the Virginia dissenters.

In Spotsylvania County on June 4, 1768, five Baptist ministers were seized by the sheriff and his deputies and brought before the court at Fredericksburg. James Childs, Lewis Craig, William Marsh, James Reed, and John Waller were charged with being disturbers of the peace. They had been preaching without authority of the local magistrates. Besides, said the prosecutor for the court, "They cannot meet a man upon a road, but they must ram a text of Scripture down his throat."

Clearly, ramming Scriptures down throats was *prima facie* evidence of breach of the peace. The magistrates set bail for each of the five at £1000 sterling, knowing full well that these poor men could not raise that amount of money. The preachers were sentenced to jail. The magistrates reported to the General Court at Williamsburg that these disturbers were "in the habit of running into private homes and making discussions."

From the jail Lewis Craig sent the Court a denial of the charges. He declared that while they were zealous in the spread of the gospel, they did not trespass on the time, property, or beliefs of other persons. Many indignant Baptists came to the jail and to the magistrates to plead for the men. The commonwealth's attorney, John Blair, felt it best to advise the release of the ministers, and after forty-five days in confinement they were freed.

Another Craig named Elijah, a Baptist preacher in Orange County, was imprisoned for illegal preaching. In 1771 Morgan Edwards of Pennsylvania, a founder of Rhode Island College, visited Virginia and wrote of Elijah Craig: "He was in Gaol at Orange for a considerable time in 1768 preaching through the bars to the people who reported to the prison, till he was confined to the inner dungeon where was no opening save a hole in the door through which he received his bread and water." [1]

Among scores, such cases as that of James Ireland of Culpeper is typical as illustrating the bitterness of the campaign against the Baptists. Ireland was an immigrant from Scotland, who felt called to preach to his Virginia neighbors. The year was 1769. The authorities ordered him to desist. Ireland later wrote:

"I sat down and counted the cost, freedom or confinement, liberty or prison? Having ventured all upon Christ, I determined to suffer all for him."

When his congregation next assembled and Ireland stood before them to preach, the constables promptly arrested him. The Culpeper magistrates sentenced him to prison. His treatment there is vividly described by Baptist historian Joseph Martin Dawson:

"The jailer, seeing the fondness of the people for the preacher, collected four shillings and eight pence from those eager to visit him. Despite weakening from cold and improper food, he preached through the bars of the small iron gate. Lurid tales persist as to swords hacking at his outstretched hands when he preached. It is recorded that in order to terrify with warnings of possible punishments to come, Negroes were cruelly whipped outside the prison where he could see and hear their distress. A plot to blow up the jail was uncovered. A physician rescued him from attempted poisoning. His tormentors burned pods of Indian pepper to smoke him to death. Yet the sturdy Scot maintained composure, continued his witness, and wrote letters to friends, headed 'From my palace in Culpeper.'

"At length the resourceful Elijah Craig procured Ireland's release. He journeyed at once to Williamsburg to appeal to the governor. Lord Botetourt received him graciously and advised how he might proceed. He returned to Culpeper for trial. The magistrates, having got wind of his favorable reception at the capital and awed by the calm of the defendant, betrayed utter confusion. He walked out of the courtroom a free man. At once he tried to resume preaching, but was too debilitated to recover his old power." [2]

Another Baptist preacher, Jeremiah Moore of Fairfax, was a special target of the establishment authorities because he had previously been an active Episcopal layman. Moore was arrested for unauthorized preaching, and in the charge committing him to the magistrates were these words: "I send you the body of Jeremiah Moore, who is a preacher of the Gospel of Jesus Christ and also a stroller."

Into Alexandria came galloping that well-known lawyer and fiery orator, Patrick Henry, to defend Preacher Moore. The vigorous advocate of religious freedom stormed into the courthouse at the beginning of Moore's trial and is quoted as saying:

"Great God, gentlemen, a man in prison for preaching the gospel of the son of God!" Henry's impassioned plea secured Moore's release.

Far from exterminating the nonconformists, or even reducing their numbers, such persecutions aroused an intense zeal among these people to secure guarantees of religious liberty.

James Madison Enters the Battle

While John Leland considered the matter of opposing Mr. Madison for the position of delegate to the Virginia Convention on Ratification, he must have recalled his friend's long record in behalf of freedom of conscience. It was young James Madison, an Episcopal student at the College of New Jersey in Princeton, who had strongly disapproved of the persecutions for religious beliefs and practices that were carried on in his native state. On January 24, 1772, he wrote from Princeton to his college friend William Bradford in Philadelphia:

"Poverty and luxury prevail among all sorts; pride, ignorance, and knavery among the priesthood; and vice and wickedness among the laity. This is bad enough; but it is not the worst I have to tell you. That diabolical, hell-conceived principle of persecution rages among some; and, to their eternal infamy, the clergy can furnish their quota of imps for such purposes. There are at this time, in the adjacent county, not less than five or six well-meaning men in close jail for publishing their religious sentiments, which in the main are very orthodox. I have neither patience to hear, talk, or think anything relative to this matter; for I have squabbled and scolded, abused and ridiculed so long about it to little purpose that I am without common patience. So I must beg you to pity me, and pray for liberty of conscience for all." [3]

After his graduation James Madison did more than write letters expressing his disapproval of religious intolerance. He appeared several times in court as a volunteer pleader in behalf of dissenters arrested for religious activities. He

became convinced that Baptists were right in their contention that government should have no control over church
affairs. Motivated by his desire to do something about this
problem, he entered active political life.

In the spring of 1776 James Madison was elected a member
of the Virginia Constitutional Convention. At twenty-five
he was its youngest delegate. In that historic convention,
youthful James Madison startled the staid gentlemen of the
establishment by offering an amendment to the Declaration
of Rights, substituting for the word *Toleration* the words
Religious Liberty. In his first speech on the floor of the
convention, Madison gave his uncomfortable elders a lecture
on the difference between toleration and liberty. Toleration,
he pointed out, presumed a favored church or religious
organization, established by governmental recognition and
deriving some of its support from the public treasury, while
permitting other sects to exist but in an inferior status.
Religious liberty, he explained, meant freedom of conscience
and worship without either governmental interference or
support. His arguments were unanswerable, and a majority
of the convention delegates voted the amendment. His arguments were also squarely in line with the Baptist position
on the matter.

The War for Independence had called men to arms.
Washington, as commander-in-chief of the Continental
Army, was fighting the British in New England. Thomas
Jefferson was a member of the Continental Congress in
Philadelphia. On July 2, 1776, the Congress passed a Decla-
ration of Independence, announced two days later, in which
Jefferson had enshrined the immortal words:

"We hold these truths to be self-evident: that all men
are created equal; that they are endowed by their Creator
with certain inalienable rights; that among these are life,

liberty and the pursuit of happinesss."

After completing his service in the Virginia Constitutional Convention of 1776, James Madison had been elected to the House of Burgesses. There he further endeared himself to the Baptists and other dissenters by successfully sponsoring a Declaration of Rights for Virginia. The statement declared that "all Citizens of the Commonwealth shall be free from coercion by the State in matters of religion." Thus the Declaration went far toward the Baptist ideal of separation of church and state.

During the war years John Leland had extended his preaching, on horseback and on foot, from Orange to Yorktown more than one hundred twenty miles away. He preached as many as a dozen sermons a week during revival services, in churches near and far, known among Baptists as "protracted meetings." Once on a June day in 1779, when his horse's back was too sore for riding, Parson Leland walked from his home to Culpeper twenty miles away, preached a funeral service and walked back home. And always he got in his vigorous licks for freedom of conscience based on the Baptist ideal that every person is "precious in the sight of the Lord" and has full authority to decide religious matters for himself.

All Leland's biographers refer to his quick wit and his good humor. One tells of an encounter Leland had with an Anglican clergyman, who challenged Leland at a meeting in which the Baptist was denouncing state support of the ministry of any church.

"The minister should get tax support so he will not have such a hard time preparing his sermons," contended the clergyman.

"But I can expound the Scriptures without any special preparation," answered Leland.

"Let's see if you can," challenged the Anglican pastor. "What, for instance, would you do with Numbers 22:21, which reads 'And Balaam . . . saddled his ass?' "

Leland gave the setting of that reference, and added: "First, Balaam, as a false prophet, represents the state-hired clergy. Second, the saddle represents the enormous tax burden of their salaries. Third, the dumb ass represents the people who bear such a tax burden!" [4]

A Victory and a New Threat

It was during that 1784 session of the General Assembly that the keen, logical persuasiveness of Madison won a majority to vote for Jefferson's Statute for Religious Freedom. The act made complete the separation of church and state in the Old Dominion and was accounted by Jefferson as one of the three great accomplishments of his career. It contained these significant words:

"Be it therefore enacted by the General Assembly, that no man shall be compelled to frequent or support any religious worship, place or ministry whatsoever, nor shall be enforced, restrained, molested, or burdened in his body or goods, nor shall otherwise suffer on account of his religious opinions or belief; but that all men shall be free to profess, and by argument to maintain, their opinions in matters of religion and that the same shall in nowise diminish, enlarge, or affect their civil capacities." [5]

Here was a tremendous victory for religious freedom, but at the very time that the battle for Jefferson's Statute for Religious Freedom was being won, another threat to spiritual liberty arose in the Old Dominion: A bill was introduced in the General Assembly to levy an assessment of taxes on all property owners for the support of teachers of religion. It provided that each taxpayer could designate the denomination or church to which his assessment would apply.

That was bad enough from the Baptist standpoint. But matters were made much worse by another section of the bill which proposed that the Protestant Episcopal Church be recognized as an incorporation by the state. There was an added stipulation that lay vestries could not remove their clergy, thus proposing to give the favored Anglican ministers a life tenure. The assessment provision applied to all sects and was a sop to gain support of the Presbyterian clergy and lay leaders, and possibly the few Methodists, to overcome the known opposition of Baptists, Catholics, and Quakers.

Sponsors of the bill, members of the old establishment, vowed they could see nothing in the provisions of this bill inconsistent with the Statute for Religious Freedom. Their argument ran thus: "The Statute forbids compulsion to support any religious worship and to believe a certain way; it grants freedom of conscience without penalty. This act is first of all a simple taxation measure for the necessary support of teachers of religion, even allowing each taxpayer his privilege to designate where his payment shall go. Secondly, in bringing order to the administration of the Anglican Church it does not interfere with complete liberty for other sects."

Persuasive arguments those—for some. But not for Baptists, nor for other dissenting sects. Nor for James Madison!

The delegate from Orange County wrote a lengthy "Memorial and Remonstrance against Assessments for Support of Religion," which was printed and widely distributed as a pamphlet. It contained these significant words: "Religion by its very nature is exempt from the authority of society at large; still less can it be subject to that of the legislative body." [6]

Virginia Baptists rallied enthusiastically to Madison's sup-

port in his fight against the bill. In a session at Dupuy's
Meeting House in Powhatan County on August 13, 1785,
their General Committee called for use of what they considered their "natural right of petition to the Government."
In their document were these words:

"Resolved, that it be recommended to those counties,
which have not yet prepared petitions to the General Assembly, against the engrossed bill for a general assessment for
the support of the teachers of the Christian religion, to
proceed in matters of religion; that no human laws ought
to be established for that purpose; but that every person
ought to be left entirely free, in respect to matters of religion:
That the Holy Author of our religion needs no such compul-
sive measures for the promotion of His cause; that the Gospel
wants not the feeble arm of man for its support: That it
has made, and will again through Divine power make its
way against opposition, and that should the Legislature
assume the right of taxing the people for the support of
the Gospel, it will be restrictive to religious liberty." [7]

Madison was impressed by the Baptist statement. He wrote
to his friend and neighbor James Monroe that although
several church groups were *for* the assessment bill, the
Baptists were "standing firmly by their avowed principle
of complete separation of church and state."

In January 1786, when the taxation bill went down to
defeat, Madison wrote to Jefferson, who was then in Paris:
"I flatter myself that we have in this country extinguished
forever the ambitious hopes of making laws for the human
mind."

"No Taxation, No Controls, No Favoritism."

Madison went on to the Constitutional Convention in
Philadelphia to assume what proved to be the major respons-

ibility in the writing of that document. By that time, Leland and his Baptist co-workers had become convinced that full religious liberty required an absolute prohibition against all legislation affecting worship, its free exercise, and its support. In correspondence with fellow Baptists in other states, especially in his native Massachusetts, Leland confirmed that his convictions on the matter were shared with growing intensity throughout the land.

In Leland's writings of that day, we find the details of the Baptist position on religious liberty, and they may be summarized thus:

First, there must be complete freedom of conscience. No one must be subject to penalties by any civil, military, or ecclesiastical authority because of religious belief or non-belief.

Second, there must be complete freedom to practice religious beliefs and activities, including the propagation of the faith at home and abroad, so long as they conform to respect for the person and the laws of human decency and safety.

Third, there must be effective separation of church and state, specifically: (a) No *taxation* in any amount for any church, religious activity, or establishment. (b) No *control* of any religious organization by an agency of the government. (c) No *favoritism* by the government toward any religious organization, whether by extending diplomatic relations or concessions to its ministers, leaders, or programs.

In several letters to Madison, the gravely concerned Leland and other crusaders for religious liberty pleaded with their friend and representative to write these cherished principles into the new constitution. Then the blow fell. Madison balked, asking for delay. Finally, in his candid and earnest manner, he declared that since the federal government was to have only delegated powers, there surely could be no opportunity for that government to abridge freedom of religion. Congress, he explained, could pass laws only on such subjects as the constitution granted it the authority to deal with. *It would have no power to legislate for or against religious liberty.*

Thus Madison had sided with Yankee John Adams, considered by Baptists as a champion of established or state-favored religion because he had declared: "Congress will never meddle with religion further than to say their own prayers, and to fast and give thanks once a year."

Leland was disappointed, but his disappointment only stirred him to further action. He wrote a pamphlet entitled "Objections to the Constitution." There were ten objections, and the first one began with these words:

"There is no Bill of Rights. Whenever a number of men enter into a state of society, a number of individual rights must be given up to society, but there should be a memorial of those not surrendered, otherwise every natural and domestic right becomes alienable, which raises Tyranny at once, and this is as necessary in one Form of Government as in another." [8]

After presenting eight other objections, Leland ended his last one by demanding protection for the people against the dangers of unrestrained political power:

"What is clearest of all—Religious Liberty, is not sufficiently secured. No religious test is required as a qualification to fill any office under the United States, but if a majority of the Congress with the President favour one system more than another, they may oblige all others to pay to the support of their system as much as they please; and if oppression does not ensue, it will be owing to the mildness of Administration, and not to any Constitutional defense, and if the manners of people are so far corrupted, that they cannot live by Republican principles, it is very dangerous leaving Religious Liberty at their mercy."

Before James Madison left Philadelphia, he had read Leland's objections and doubtless had studied them carefully. Was Leland right? Was there danger, despite the specific delegation of powers which began with "Congress shall have power," that any human liberties could be infringed? The convention was drawing to a close, so what could be done now? Such questions must have given Madison careful thought.

Just as the convention ended, a letter came to Madison from James Gordon, Jr., of Orange, informing him that several men of the county were contemplating filing their names for delegate of the Convention on Ratification, with the announced purpose of opposing ratification. One of these, the letter said, was Colonel Charles Barbour; in addition, Parsons Bledsoe and Leland, with Col. Z. Burnley, were all opposed.

Another letter, this one from Captain Joseph Spencer, a Baptist who had served time in prison for his religious faith, discussed the rising tide of opposition to the constitution, and added: "Mr. Leeland and Mr. Bledsoe and Sanders are the most publick men of the society in Orange, therefor as Mr. Leeland lyes in your way home from Fredericksburg to Orange would advise you to call on him and spend a few hours in his company . . ." [9]

Meeting Under Oak Trees

Some of Leland's biographers give considerable credit to Sallie Leland, that devout and spirited woman who had counseled her husband on every move he made after their marriage, for suggesting the solution to the problem of how

John might gain his purpose without going to the Convention. Others give the major credit to Colonel Barbour. It seems certain that Sallie did not want to be left alone with their brood of children while John attended a long-winded convention. It is certain that the Colonel, at the Goochland meeting in March 1788, offered to withdraw if Leland would announce for the position.

Perhaps both the wife and the close friend advised John to strike a bargain with Madison. The new constitution provided for amendments. If Madison would agree to be a member of the First Congress and present amendments that the Baptists wanted, John could announce that he would not run for delegate to the convention and would support James Madison.

Madison stopped at Mount Vernon overnight to visit the Washingtons, then hurried on to Fredericksburg. There he was warned by several friends and supporters that he would have a hard time being elected a delegate to the convention unless he gained the support of the influential Baptist leader.

With John Leland's "Objections to the Constitution" in his pocket, Mr. Madison dismounted from his carriage at the front door of the Leland farm home. After the greetings and pleasantries were exchanged, Madison and his host excused themselves from Sallie and the children and strolled out into the side yard. There, under the great oak trees, the two men talked earnestly.

Madison still had to be convinced that additional guarantees of religious liberty and other freedoms mentioned in the Objections were necessary. Leland brought all his persuasive power to bear upon his distinguished friend. Apparently, no record of their conversation was ever made, but soon afterward Candidate James Madison spoke to a picnic crowd in an oak grove near Gum Spring, six miles from Orange. Standing on a hogshead of tobacco so he could be easily seen and heard, he told his listeners that he would indeed run for the First Congress and if elected, would introduce the amendments suggested by the Rev. Mr. Leland and many honest and intelligent citizens.

Once committed to the task of formulating amendments, James Madison became engrossed in the work. As an elected member of the First Congress, he consulted farmers, merchants, lawyers, editors. He reported occasionally to George Washington, who heartily approved the idea of what Madison called a "Bill of Rights." He carefully considered such pleas as these:

"Let no one be imprisoned for saying or printing his opinions!"

"The British put their soldiers in our home without our consent!"

"Mr. Madison, let it be writ that no official can take property without just payment."

"Let no constable search my house without a warrant!"

And of course he consulted Preacher Leland, who had one firm request: "Let freedom of religion lead all the rest in the Bill of Rights."

On January 2, 1789, Madison wrote to the Rev. George Eve, pastor of the Blue Run Baptist Church in Orange County: "Circumstances have now changed. It is my sincere opinion that the Constitution ought to be revised, and that the first Congress . . . ought to prepare and recommend to the States for ratification the most satisfactory provisions for essential rights, particularly the rights of conscience in the fullest latitude, the freedom of the press, trials by jury, security against general warrants, etc." [10]

One afternoon early in that first session of the Congress, all eyes in the House of Representatives were turned toward the small man with sparse dark hair and piercing gray eyes, as James Madison stood and announced:

"Mr. Speaker, I have the honor to present for the consideration of this body certain proposed amendments to the constitution of the United States. I shall read them. The first one states:

" 'Congress shall make no law respecting an establishment of religion, or prohibiting the free exercise thereof; or abridging the freedom of speech, or of the press, or of the right of the people peaceably to assemble, and to petition the government for a redress of grievances.' "

The Bill of Rights had started on its way to adoption.

2

ROGER WILLIAMS

*The Baptist Who Befriended Persons
"Distressed of Conscience"*

The man destined to found the first Baptist church on American soil, Roger Williams, was born probably in late 1603. It was the year in which Elizabeth, known as Good Queen Bess, having reigned for two generations, passed from mortal life, and James I was proclaimed King.

Roger Williams' birthplace is in dispute. It is known that his parents lived for a time in Wales, and some church historians believe that Roger was born in that British principality. The weight of evidence favors the conclusion that the Williamses were living in London from about 1600 and that Roger was born there. It is certain from his own writings that he worked at his father's tailor-merchant shop as a boy.

The Williams' home was near the square in front of Newgate Prison, the favorite site of the authorities for the execution of condemned heretics. As a lad, Roger witnessed many such executions. The people in the crowds who came to take in the ghastly spectacles generally considered them a time for laughing, mocking, and jeering at the condemned wretches. Roger, however, developed a sense of pity which grew to shame and abhorrence at such inhumanity toward persons whose only crime in many instances was nonconformity in matters of conscience.

It was through his mother's side of the family, rather than his father's, that young Roger Williams came in close contact with persons of political influence in England. His mother was of the prominent Pembertons, close friends of Sir Edward Coke, a liberal-minded lawyer and jurist. Noting Roger's exceptional talents, Sir Edward placed him under a master who taught the lad to take shorthand notes. When Roger was eighteen years old, Coke secured a scholarship for him at the Charter House. Appointed to the King's Bench as chief justice, Sir Edward employed young Williams to record the proceedings in the Court of the Star Chamber.

Day after day, there came before the Star Chamber court for trial the men, women, and, frequently, young children accused of crimes. Roger Williams heard and transcribed all the arguments in use against those considered heretical criminals. The injustice of punishing persons who refused to believe religious dogma prescribed by the state developed in the young man an intense hatred of bigotry and intolerance. He rebelled against the practice of denying freedom of conscience.

Sir Edward continued to sponsor Roger Williams through Pembroke College, Cambridge, from which the young man was graduated in 1627. While a student, Williams followed with keen interest the debates and discussions between his sponsor, Sir Edward, and William Laud, Bishop of London and later Archbishop of Canterbury, who was an implacable enemy of the Puritans, Calvinists, and all other nonconformists. Bishop Laud, a high churchman, restored many of the rites and ceremonies of Roman Catholicism; Coke firmly opposed such moves. Roger Williams sided with the point of view of his patron, writing and speaking for the Puritan cause.

Williams took two years of postgraduate work at Cambridge, studying for the ministry, mastering Latin, Greek, and Hebrew, and becoming proficient also in Dutch and French. By the time he left the university he was recognized as an eloquent young preacher, a forceful debater, an ardent rebel against conformity in religion. He served as a chaplain in the home of Sir William Masham for a time, and this position brought him in touch with such men as Oliver Cromwell and John Hampden.

Chaplain Williams proposed to a young lady of noble birth, but when the family refused to allow the union, Williams married a maid in the Masham household, Mary Barnard. His friends severely criticized him for marrying beneath his station, but Mary proved a staunch and loyal companion during the turbulent years they lived and labored together.

With dismay, Roger Williams saw his sponsor, Sir Edward Coke, degraded and sent to prison in the Tower of London by King James. And worse days lay ahead after King Charles I succeeded King James in 1625. Autocratic and contemptuous of Parliament and democratic procedures, Charles gave full rein to Archbishop Laud to persecute the Puritans and other dissenters. By 1630 the campaign to exterminate nonconformists reached a high pitch. Numerous dissenters were imprisoned and punished by fines and mutilation, sometimes by execution. With burning indignation Williams witnessed the cruel treatment assessed against Dr. Alexander Leighton, a minister who had become an influential Puritan and had written a protest entitled *Zion's Plea Against the Prelacy*, which was critical of the intolerance of established church leaders. For this offense he was arrested on Archbishop Laud's orders, and the bishop stipulated in detail the following punishment:

"Committed to the Prison of the Fleet for Life, and pay a fine of ten thousand pounds; that the High Commission should degrade him from his ministry; and that he should be brought to the pillory at Westminster while the Court is sitting and be publicly whipped; after whipping be set upon a pillory a convenient time and have one of his ears cut off, one side of his nose split, and be branded in the face with a double SS for a sower of sedition; then that he should be carried back to prison, and after a few days be pilloried a second time in Cheapside, and have the other side of his nose split and his other ear cut off, and then be shut up in close prison for the rest of his life." [1]

Roger Williams decided that the time had come to fight such shocking punishments for differences in religious opinions, regardless of the consequences to himself. He identified himself with the Separatists-Baptists and penned a moving protest called *Dissent*. Addressed to Archbishop Laud, it voiced in forceful words his undying opposition to all religious intolerance.

Williams' thinking on the vital issue of religious liberty was strongly influenced by a most tragic, senseless, destructive conflict that began in 1618 and was to rage over many areas of Germany and Bohemia until 1648, the Thirty Years' War. The causes lay deep in the rivalries of European rulers and their determination to maintain the religion that they favored. It was indeed a conflict to the death between Catholics and Protestants, a struggle for supremacy of princes loyal to Rome against princes supporting Luther and the Reformation. Along with all intelligent and thoughtful English Separatists, Roger Williams became increasingly confirmed in the belief that the combination of church and state resulted in coercion, persecution, and conflict of the type then raging in middle Europe; and that only separation of church and state could prevent such evils in the future.

Exile in America

Williams' *Dissent* produced the inevitable result. Laud ordered that the defiant author be seized and brought to trial forthwith. However, Roger Williams had come to a calm decision. He would not become a victim to the spleen of this church leader and the pliant monarch. He would preserve his life and continue his fight for religious freedom.

Many Separatists, particularly Baptists and Quakers, had fled to Holland. Williams decided that he, too, would become an exile from his native land. But he would not go to Holland. He had received an urgent invitation from the church of the Puritans in Boston to migrate to that city and preach to their congregation. Considering this a providential opportunity, Williams embarked secretly on a ship sailing for America on December 8, 1630. It was the *Lyon*, putting out from Bristol and bound for Boston. By Roger's side was his wife Mary, as eager as he to begin a new life in a new world.

In the diary of Governor John Winthrop of Massachusetts under the date February 5, 1631, there is an entry that tells of his welcoming the good ship *Lyon*, arrived at Boston Harbor with its twenty passengers. His Excellency the Governor mentioned four of these passengers by name, and two of these were "Mr. Williams (a godly minister) with his wife."

It had been a long, stormy voyage, and Roger and Mary Williams were heartily glad to set foot on land. Along with Governor Winthrop, several other important church leaders in the Massachusetts Bay Colony were waiting to welcome the still-young man. They had heard of his eloquent preaching in England and of his becoming an exile to escape the rigid conformity that King Charles insisted upon. There was an acute shortage of trained preachers among the Boston Puritans. Surely this tall, intelligent, handsome, 28-year-old minister was the answer to their prayers.

Hardly had Roger Williams found lodgings for himself and his wife when he began to inquire thoughtfully into the exact doctrines and practices of the Massachusetts Bay Puritans. He had supposed that the sep~ration of three thousand miles of ocean, if no other factor, had given them freedom to separate from the rigid beliefs of their Puritanical leaders in the homeland. He discovered that like their cousins in England, these Puritans clung to the principle that the government must insure the financial support of an established church and, more important, must protect that church from error. Williams was staunchly opposed to this view.

Doubtless, Williams understood the fundamental reasons for Puritan intolerance. He must have learned that the Puritan mind held tenaciously to a train of reasoning which seemed to that mind to be the soul of logic, the essence of unquestionable truth, namely: The Scriptures are the source of all authority for creed and practice. The Scriptures are clear and plain, the answer to every problem and situation, spiritual or civil. It is the responsibility of the minister, as Christ's spokesman, to interpret the Holy Writ. If any person does not agree with the interpretation, he is obviously in error; it is then the duty of the minister to dispute with him and correct the error. If the person still does not agree, it is because he stubbornly holds to his error and, like an erring child, must be punished until he forsakes his error. So that the church might not suffer from persistent error, the state must help the church force the truth upon the person by proper punishment.

The Massachusetts colony was in fact a mixture of democracy and theocracy, in which civil and religious laws were

so intermingled as to be inseparable. These Puritans called
their state the Holy Commonwealth. Roger Williams had
pulled far away from belief in such a church-state rela-
tionship before leaving England. He had every intention
of carrying a torch for freedom of conscience in the new
land, a land that he had supposed would be receptive to
the encouragement of spiritual liberty.

Assuming that Roger Williams would be honored to serve
them as pastor-teacher, the Boston Puritan leaders formally
offered him the position. They had not counted on Williams'
hardening conviction against any and all control of religious
affairs by what he called the civil power. He shocked them
by refusing the offer and by his explanation: "I durst not
officiate to an unseparated people."

The Boston Puritans considered themselves separated
enough and looked upon Williams' announcement as insult-
ing. They marked him as a man to be dealt with firmly
in due course of time.

Thundering from Salem

Roger and Mary visited among churchgoers of other communities of the Massachusetts Bay settlers. At Salem they
found a neighborhood of independent thinkers who had
emigrated from England in 1628 and had separated from
the Boston Puritans for precisely the same reasons Williams
refused to become the Boston teacher: They refused to
accept the idea of public control over conscience and worship. They were, in his opinion, a true congregational type
of church. The vigorous young minister preached for them,
and the members liked him. They called him to be their
teacher, and he accepted. He found keen satisfaction in
preaching and lecturing to a people who supported his
doctrine that the authority of the state, whether in Boston

or in London, lay only in civil affairs.

"According to Divine Law," Williams proclaimed in his sermons, "officers of the Crown cannot rightfully interfere with the right of a person to worship as he pleases!" He even carried his argument to the conclusion that magistrates were without the right to punish Sabbath-breaking, swearing, and other violations of the first four of the Ten Commandments, since those matters were in the realm of the spiritual. As though to answer this brash young preacher, the General Court of the Massachusetts Bay Colony, the legislative group for the settlers, on May 18, 1631, passed an ordinance that stated:

"Noe man shall be admitted to the freedom of this body politicke, but such as are members of some of the churches within the limits of the same." Williams roared back that there could be no true freedom without freedom of conscience to join a church or not to join a church as one might please. Such teachings shocked and angered the Boston Puritans. Here was heresy of the rankest kind.

Perhaps an even greater offense on the part of Parson Williams alarmed the smug and strait-laced fathers of the colony. Williams went out among the Narragansett Indians, from whom the land of the colony had been purchased, and told them of the Great Spirit. He told the Indians that this Great Spirit was the creator and father of all mankind, and that like a father he cared for his children. Furthermore, the earnest evangelist declared, the Great Spirit wanted men to treat one another as brothers.

This was bad enough, so far as the Calvinistic Puritans were concerned, for surely none of these aborigines could be counted as among God's elect and so to preach to them was foolish and futile. But even more disconcerting was Williams' discovery that the Narragansett tribe had been paid only a pittance for the land of the colonists. In this nosey preacher's view, the Indians had been swindled by people supposed to be pure of heart.

After six months at Salem, harassed and threatened with arrest and punishment, Roger Williams and his wife found refuge at Plymouth among the Pilgrim separatists, who were much more humane in religious views than were the Puritans. There the Williamses remained for nearly two years, while Roger served the congregation as assistant pastor. Governor William Bradford was a regular worshiper in the Plymouth congregation and highly esteemed this fiery young minister and his independent views.

Williams again went out to the Indians, the Massasoits, to make friends and to teach the Christian gospel. Again he was received gladly. The chiefs and their braves were delighted to find a paleface who met them as a brother and spoke of all being children of the Great Spirit. Williams actually drafted a treaty of friendship with the Massasoit tribe, which was to serve as an important item in his establishment of his own colony.

Despite their stand that a government should not force religion upon anyone, the Pilgrims believed in the support of the church by the government. Unable to change their views, Williams became restless at Plymouth. In the summer of 1633 he received an official call from the congregation at Salem to return as the pastor. He gladly accepted, and back to Salem came Roger and Mary Williams. Soon afterward their first child, a son, was born.

Now the battle between the Boston Puritans and this contentious young minister began in earnest, as Williams grew more outspoken against religious intolerance and the authorities grew more determined to silence him.

"I affirm that there was never civil state in the world

that ever did or ever shall make good work of it, with a civil sword in spiritual matters," he declared in a vigorous sermon that he defiantly published. He chided the religious leaders for using the civil authorities to carry out their persecutions, charging that "under a pretense of holy orders in themselves, they put over a drudgery of execution to their enslaved seculars." [2]

"The state should give an absolute permission of conscience to all men in what is spiritual!" was the theme of many a Williams discourse.

It seems certain that Roger Williams' rebellious attitude was a principal reason for the passage by the General Court, on May 14, 1634, of a Freeman's Oath. It specifically provided for "the right of Magistrates to punish for breaches of the First Table (of the Ten Commandments) and to rule in religion." The clear purpose of this act was to eradicate all opposition to the Holy Commonwealth in both civil and religious matters. It required all men to take an oath of loyalty to the General Court. Failure or refusal to do so was punishable by banishment.

Parson Williams Goes to Trial

Williams promptly accepted this new challenge. He vehemently attacked the act as both illegal and unjust, and was served with a summons for trial on the charge of "entertaining dangerous opinions." Even Governor John Endicott, who had befriended Williams in the past, agreed that the trial should be held.

The court assembled in Boston on October 8, 1635. It was composed of all the magistrates of the colony, who were at the same time the complaining witnesses, the prosecutors, the jury, and the judges. Sitting among them as advisers to the court were Puritan ministers, the principal witnesses against the culprit. Williams had no legal defender, as no one learned in the law dared volunteer as his counsel for fear of reprisals.

The complaints were heard, one after another, with quotations from Williams' speeches and sermons to prove the charge of "dangerous opinions," which in themselves constituted sedition against the Holy Commonwealth. When Williams rose to his own defense, he startled the court with his calm but forceful words. All that he had learned in his reporting days in the Court of the Star Chamber in London came back to help him now. He remained respectful and courteous throughout the long day and into the night of the trial, quoting Scripture to combat the accusations of sedition. He declared his support of the Ten Commandments, but remained firm in his opinion that the First Table was not to be enforced by the civil power. He actually won several of the magistrates to his viewpoint, and they refused to vote for his conviction.

But the Puritan advisers were constantly at the elbows of the magistrates, urging them to do their duty for the peace and quiet of the community, and the result was a foregone conclusion: a sentence of banishment from the Massachusetts Bay Colony. However, Williams was given an opportunity to recant and to announce his decision on the next day. When the court reassembled to hear if he would recant, Williams declared: "I shall be ready . . . not only to be bound and banished, but to die also in New England for my convictions and for the truth as I see it!"

Refuge Among the Indians

Roger Williams returned to his home and his wife and child. The court had allowed him six weeks to prepare to leave the colony. He stayed close to Salem, plotting how he might outwit the Puritan ministers and their helpers, the magistrates. Many friends came to visit him, usually at night, to offer sympathy and wish the family well.

Among the visitors was Henry Vane, Jr., son of Sir Henry Vane of London, one of England's outstanding statesmen of that day. The young man was impressed with Williams' sincerity and deplored his banishment. Vane's visit began a friendship that stood the dissenting parson in good stead in later years.

One day a close friend brought Williams a secret message from Governor Winthrop. The Boston authorities were planning to seize Williams and put him aboard a ship bound for England, the message said. Again Williams decided he would not be a martyr if he could escape and continue his fight for liberty of conscience. That night he bundled himself in his greatcoat, stuffed some food into his pockets, kissed his wife and baby good-by, and stole out into the darkness.

A storm was blowing up and by midnight it had turned into a blizzard. Williams headed southwestward toward Narragansett Bay, shuffling along the drifting snow over fields and through forests. It grew bitter cold and the wind howled and shrieked about him. During the next day, utterly exhausted and nearly frozen, he reached a camp of the Narragansett Indians. Greeting him as a brother, these friends took him in, fed him, thawed him out, and insisted that he remain in hiding with them.

Through all the rest of that winter the exiled minister stayed with his Indian benefactors, sharing their food and their shelter, telling them more about the Great Spirit. A quarrel developed between two rival chieftains, and war was about to begin when Williams traveled from one chief to the other, urging them to keep the peace. He brought the tribal leaders together and the quarrel was settled. In gratitude, Chief Massasoit gave Williams a tract of land on the east bank of the Seekonk River.

During the winter the exiled parson had made a momentous decision. He would establish his own colony, and it would be open to all who wanted to live in the enjoyment of religious freedom. The gift of land from Chief Massasoit seemed just the place for such a settlement and Williams began to build a house and plant a field there. Governor Winthrop of Plymouth advised him that he was on land of the Massachusetts Bay Colony, and it would be safer if he moved, as Williams later wrote, "to the other side of the water, and then, he said, I had the country free as themselves and we should be loving neighbors together." [3]

A Village Called Providence

By this time several of Williams' Salem friends had joined him, and the small group moved across to the west side of the Mooshassuc River. There Williams bought land from the Indians and began laying out a village which he called Providence. His family joined him in their new home, and there the second child was born, a daughter whom Mary named Freeborn.

Roger Williams invited settlers to come to his "Providence Plantations," making it clear that he had set up "a shelter for persons distressed for conscience." The colony, he announced, would have a civil government with no authority over religious matters. All who came could worship in their own way, if they cared to, or be free not to worship.

The settlers came, singly and in families. There were dissenters from Boston and other areas of the Massachusetts colony; Quakers from communities where they had been persecuted by Puritans and Congregationalists; a few families of Jews from New Amsterdam, fleeing the discriminations and harassments of the Dutch.

With high satisfaction Roger Williams watched this experiment for three years, then decided to organize his own church. It would be a congregation based upon the Anabaptist principles of the churches of John Smyth and Thomas Helwys in Holland and England. It would be a church of baptized believers, with immersion the symbol of death to sin and resurrection to a new life.

One day in March about a dozen men and women assembled at the Williams home. In the chilly waters of a nearby stream Roger Williams had himself immersed by Ezekiel Holliman, who had been a member of the Salem church; then Williams baptized Holliman and the others. Thus was organized the Providence Baptist Church, the first Baptist church on American soil, and still in honored existence.

Just as he had opened the door of his colony for all to enjoy religious liberty, so Roger Williams opened his church for any to come and worship who wished to do so. The congregation held services in the Williams home until a meeting house was built. The founder and pastor made it a point to inform his neighbors that they were welcome not only to worship with his congregation but also to join the fellowship if, as he put it, they were "like-minded" in the Baptist faith.

The Rhode Island Compact

Roger Williams became assailed with doubts as to the validity of his own baptism. While he left no specific record of those doubts, his ruggedly honest nature prompted him to resign from the pastorate and the membership of his church in July, 1640. All the remainder of his life Williams termed himself a "seeker."

But Roger Williams never repudiated or denied any Baptist principles which he had embraced when he assembled his congregation. Rather, he emphasized his belief in them, in Rhode Island, and later in England during his stay in his native land as he worked to obtain a charter for his colony. In fact, Williams went the whole distance for complete religious liberty. To qualify as a citizen of Rhode Island one signed a compact of tremendous historic significance in the development of the separation of church and state in America. In the simple language of the common man it read:

"We whose names are hereunder written, being desirous to inhabit the town of Providence, do promise to submit ourselves in active or passive obedience to all such orders or agreements as shall be made for the public good of the body, in an orderly way, by the major consent of the present inhabitants, masters of families incorporated together in a township, and such others when they shall admit into the same, only in civil things."

Surely none who signed the compact, including the founder himself, could have foreseen that in less than one and one-half centuries the principle embodied in those four words, *only in civil things,* would be accepted as part of the fundamental law of the new union of states and written into the constitutions of its various commonwealths.

Roger Williams was not content merely to see that spiritual liberty was guaranteed in the citizens' compact and in Rhode Island's laws. He stood by vigilantly to insure that his principles were followed and enforced. On several occasions the matter of the interpretation of religious liberty came to the test.

"Should not our council pass a Sunday-observance law, as enacted by the Puritans, since it is man's duty to rest on the Sabbath?" was asked and discussed among the settlers. Williams' answer was a definite "No!" This was a matter of conscience, he said, so long as the citizen obeyed the civil laws on Sunday as on all other days. No compulsory Sunday-observance act was ever enacted in Rhode Island while Williams lived, nor any other law relating to duties that a man might owe to God.

"What about such heretics as Seventh Day Baptists, who defy the accepted Christian concept of worshiping on Sunday and insist upon observing Saturday as the day of rest and worship?" was asked. Here again Williams asserted that this was a matter of conscience, and even though the practice of worshiping on the seventh day ran counter to the majority in the community, the religious minority, however small, should not be troubled for their beliefs. He welcomed these seventh-day worshipers, who were persecuted and discriminated against in almost every other American colony, and they came in such numbers that in 1671 they organized a conference. Later, one of their faith served as governor of the state.

Records of the colony show that one of the settlers, Joshua Verin, "restrained his wife from going to meeting as often as she desired." Whether Mrs. Verin's plaint was based upon sound reasons or whether it might indicate unmentioned domestic difficulties is not known. However, Joshua Verin was "withheld from liberty of voting in the Council until he shall declare to the contrary," which meant until he agreed to let his good wife go to meeting without interference even from her husband. Thus Williams and his band of believers in freedom of conscience and worship struggled to establish their community.

Williams versus Cotton

It is difficult for modern minds, accustomed to freedom

of conscience and worship, to grasp how generally accepted
was the belief that the union of church and state was necessary in order to insure conformity in religious affairs in the
period of American colonial history. The feeling was tersely
expressed by a Boston attorney, Nathanial Ward, who styled
himself "Lawyer Divine," presumably because he was the
legal representative of the established church. Ward had
drawn up the church and civil rules that were the first legal
code for the community. In discussing Williams' argument
that no one should be forced to believe or practice religion
in a prescribed manner, Ward exclaimed: "It is an astonish-
ment to think that the brains of men should be parboiled
in such impious ignorance!"

Such criticism failed to shake Roger Williams' firm belief
in the principle of complete spiritual liberty. When he was
accused by Boston's outstanding Puritan minister, John Cotton, of encouraging anarchy and discouraging the progress
of Christianity by his stand against control of religion by
the state, Williams answered with this illustration:

"There goes many a ship to sea, with many hundred souls
on one ship, whose weal and woe is common, and is a true
picture of a commonwealth, or a human combination or
society. It hath fallen out sometimes that both Baptists and
Protestants, Jews and Turks, may be embarked into one ship;
upon which supposal I do affirm that all the liberty of
conscience that ever I pleaded for turns upon these two
things; that none of the Baptists, Protestants, Jews or Turks
be forced to come to the ship's prayers or worship; nor
secondly, be compelled from their own particular prayers
or worship."

In 1643 Williams sailed for London to obtain an official
charter for his colony, so that it could be secure from enemies
within and without. Sir Henry Vane was now a member
of Parliament and volunteered to help smooth the way for

consideration of Williams' request. Even so, the ponderous bureaucracy of the Crown's government consumed several months as Williams was sent from one influential official to another, finding them in greater haste to go fox hunting than to concern themselves with a small colony in far-off America led by a dissenting parson.

While waiting for action on his request, Williams' restless spirit prompted him to write a lengthy discussion entitled *The Bloudy (Bloody) Tenet of Persecution for Cause of Conscience*. In this work he summarized all his arguments showing the danger to human liberties flowing from state control of religion. In the quaint, stilted English of his day, flavored with his wordy but expressive language, the champion of freedom denounced compulsion of mind and conscience in spiritual matters.

"It is the will of God," he wrote, "that since the coming of his Sonne the Lord Jesus, a permission of the most Paganish, Jewish, Turkish, or Antichristian consciences and worships, bee granted to all men in all Nations and Countries: and they are onley to bee fought against with that Sword which is onely (in Soule matters) able to conquer, to wit, the Sword of God's spirit, the Worde of God. True civility and Christianity may both flourish in a state or Kingdome, notwithstanding the permission of divers and contrary consciences, either of Jew or Gentile."

John Cotton took on the task of debating with Williams in what turned out to be a long exchange of letters and statements. The Bay Colony's most ardent exponent of the control of religion by the state brought out the usual arguments favoring the enforcement of the authority of an established church upon all the population under its jurisdiction, while Williams parried every thrust of the learned theologian with the sharp blade of his own arguments in behalf of complete liberty. Their historic discussions may be summarized:

Cotton: "It is a carnal and worldly, and indeed an ungodly imagination, to confine the magistrate's charge to the bodies and goods of the subject, and to exclude them from the care of their souls."

Williams: "If it be the magistrate's duty or office, then is he both a temporal and ecclesiastical officer: the contrary to which most men will affirm. That doctrine and distinction, that a magistrate may punish a heretic civilly, will not here avail."

The Charter Is Secured

Williams felt that he had the plain lessons of history to support his contention that the union of church and state, with enforcement of established religion and beliefs, resulted in countless injustices and widespread tyranny. He condensed much English history with the remark that the realm had been filled with blood and confusion for a hundred years and this explanation:

"Henry the Seventh leaves England under the slavish bondage of the Pope's yoke. Henry the Eighth reforms all England to a new fashion, half Papist, half Protestant. King Edward the Sixth turns about the wheels of state, and works the whole land to absolute Protestantism. Queen Mary, succeeding to the helm, steers a direct contrary course, breaks in pieces all that Edward wrought, and brings forth an old edition of England's reformation, all Popish. Mary not living out half her days, Elizabeth, like Joseph, is advanced from the prison to the palace, and from the irons to the crown; she plucks up all her sister Mary's plants, and sounds a trumpet, all Protestant. What sober man is not amazed at these revolutions!" [4]

Roger Williams' patience, with the help of Sir Henry Vane's influence with members of Parliament, finally won out. On March 14, 1644, the charter for The Rhode Island and Providence Plantations was granted by the Parliamentary Board for Commissioners for Plantations. In triumph the founder brought back to Providence his cherished patent, and in triumph he was welcomed home by his fellow colonists. The charter defined the boundaries of the small colony and gave the settlers the power to form their own government, elect all their officers, and make all their laws. Williams was promptly given the title of president of the colony.

Firmly embodied in the Rhode Island charter was the principle of government of, by, and for the people. All persons in the colony (male, and over twenty-one years of age, of course) were given an equal voice in the government if they were law-abiding and peaceful men. Williams expressed his principle of rule by the people in these words:

"The Civill Power is originally and fundamentally in the People . . . a People may erect and establish what forme of Government seemes to them most meete for their civill condition: It is evident that such Governments as are by them erected and established, have no more power, nor for a longer time, than the civill power of people consenting and agreeing shall betrust them with. This is cleere not only in Reason, but in the experience of all commonweales, where the people are not deprived of their naturall freedome by the power of Tyrants."

The Rhode Island settlers' nonconformity brought down upon them the contempt of officials and members of other American colonies. This situation was well illustrated when a ship bearing Quakers fleeing the persecutions of England and the Netherlands docked at New Amsterdam. The master of this Dutch port refused to allow these strange persons, who would not bear arms and tended to shut themselves up within the enclosure of their own people, to embark. He recorded:

"We suppose they went to Rhode Island, for that is the receptacle of all sorts of riffraff people, and is nothing else than the sewer of New England. All the cranks of New England retire thither. We suppose they will settle there, as they are not tolerated by the Independents in any other place."

The Quakers on that ship did settle there, and so did other shiploads of Quakers. They were generally as contentious in religious doctrines as was Williams himself, and were a source of irritation to the founder. But Williams showed his opposition to their debates with their leaders and let the people judge as to which side had the truth.

Williams maintained his close friendship with the Indians, even learning their tribal languages. He wrote a brief Narragansett dictionary and also a Key to other Indian dialects. "It was not price nor money that could have purchased Rhode Island; Rhode Island was purchased by love," he said.

Once a townsman missed six of his cows and demanded that the Providence officials declare war on the thieving Indians. Williams investigated and found that some Indian children playing near the pasture had frightened the herd. The parson went to the chief of the tribe and stated the trouble. Together the two men searched the woods until the lost cattle were rounded up and returned.

When agents of the Massachusetts Bay Colony needed an interpreter for some important treaty negotiations with the Narragansett chiefs, they chose Roger Williams, the man they had banished, to entrust with this responsibility.

In the years that followed the life and work of the founder of the first Baptist church in America, some Baptists have severely criticized Roger Williams for his leaving the Baptist fellowship and becoming a seeker. Other Baptists are more charitable, pointing out that he never swerved from his belief in spiritual liberty and all other historic Baptist principles. They point out, also, that Williams' becoming a seeker only exemplified his rugged spiritual honesty when assailed by doubts about the wisdom of continuing his own spiritual leadership as pastor.

3

JOHN CLARKE
*The Baptist Who Wrested a Charter
of Freedom from King Charles*

In establishing Rhode Island as a haven of religious freedom among the American colonies, the name of John Clarke
must be written beside that of Roger Williams. This well-
educated, free-thinking young English immigrant was born
in London in 1609. Apprenticed to a doctor, John became
a skillful physician. He was also an earnest student of law
and theology.

Clarke became a dissenter from the Anglican Church, and
to avoid persecution he lived for a time in Leyden, Holland,
where he came in contact with the Baptists, although he
did not join their fellowship in that city.

The Condemnation of Anne Hutchinson

Hoping to find freedom of conscience and a profitable
new life in America, Clarke sailed for Boston in November,
1637. He reached the Massachusetts Bay capital in time
for a rude shock. The town was all stirred up over the
teachings of a cultured, independent-thinking woman, Anne
Hutchinson. The mother of fourteen children, she was at-
tracting wide attention by holding religious discussion meetings in her home every Thursday evening. At these gatherings

she would encourage anyone to express his or her opinion on spiritual matters, and would lead discussions on subjects supposed not to be open to diversity of opinions, such as the meaning of the Scriptures, the way of salvation, and the duties of the Christian life.

Not all Anne Hutchinson's ideas and beliefs conformed to the Puritan way of thought and practice, so the Boston authorities became alarmed at her influence and the possibility that she might lead some of the parishioners astray. The Puritan elders drew up a long list of what they called erroneous opinions this woman was accused of holding and called her to appear for an accounting. She came and stood fearlessly before her inquisitors, answering their questions and refuting their accusations, often by quoting Scripture. Some days later she was denounced openly, at a worship service in the Puritan Meeting House, by the leading elder of the city, John Wilson. From the pulpit of his church Wilson thundered:

"I denounce you, Anne Hutchinson, in the house of God, as a woman of dangerous and heretical errors. I denounce you as a servant of Satan. I cast you out as a leper that you no more blaspheme, seduce, and lie. I do order the congregation to treat you as a heathen and publican!" [1]

Anne Hutchinson turned and walked slowly out of the meeting house. Before she reached the door a small lass, Mary Dyer, sprang up, ran to her side, and walked out with her, an act of childlike kindness that enraged the righteous Puritan elders. It was a crime for any person to help or give comfort to a branded heretic.

"The girl must pay for this!" the elders vowed. Mary Dyer did pay for her deed, and for many other actions which showed her devotion to humanity. She became a follower of the contentious Quakers and publicly defended their beliefs. On a spring afternoon, twenty-four years after the Anne Hutchinson incident, Mary Dyer was led to the Boston Common with hands chained and legs shackled as a criminal, charged with being a "vile Quakeress," and from a rude scaffold she was hanged by the neck until dead.

Anne Hutchinson left Boston and the Massachusetts Bay Colony in late 1638 and with several of her younger children fled to the shelter of Roger Williams' Providence community.

The Founders of Newport

The persecution of Anne Hutchinson sickened John Clarke. He wrote in his diary: "A year in this hotbed of religious tyranny is enough for me. I cannot bear to see men in these uttermost parts of the earth not able to bear with others in matters of conscience and live peaceable together. With so much land before us, I for one will turn aside, shake the dust of Boston off my feet, and betake me to a new place. There I shall make a haven for all those who, like myself, are disgusted and sickened by the Puritan dictatorship. I shall make it a place where there will be full freedom of thought and religious conscience."

The only place affording freedom of thought and religious conscience was Providence town and plantations. To that haven John Clarke and several of his associates went, and there they were greeted and welcomed by Roger Williams, who helped Clarke and his small band of freedom seekers to purchase from the Indians a pleasant coastal island called Aquidneck in Narragansett Bay. There Clarke started his settlement and town, which he named Newport.

In 1640 Clarke and several of his colonists announced themselves as professed dissenters, and during that year they organized the First Baptist Church of Newport, the second Baptist church on American soil. John Clarke became the minister and continued as pastor and leader until his death in 1676.

It is not certain from the records whether John Clarke adopted immersion for the baptism of believers who formed his congregation or who joined it soon after its founding. In 1644 Mark Lukar, an English Separatist who had been immersed two years previously and immigrated to America soon afterward, joined Clarke's colony and church. Lukar's influence seems to have been the deciding factor in the acceptance by Clarke and his congregation of immersion as the official mode of baptism, as it was for the First Baptist Church of Providence.

John Clarke was inspired with missionary zeal, and occasionally left Rhode Island to preach for Separatist and other dissenting congregations in Massachusetts. In 1649 he attempted with the help of one of his most active laymen, Obadiah Holmes, to organize a Baptist church at Seekonk, Massachusetts, but he and his helpers were thwarted by the authorities.

Obadiah Holmes succeeded John Clarke as pastor of Newport Church. He had immigrated from England, settling in Salem, where he set up the first glassworks on American soil. He joined the Congregational church at Salem, but after some years he moved to Rehoboth in the Plymouth colony. Deciding against the presbyterial type of Puritan control he became a Separatist, and gathered a small band of like-minded people for worship. For this step he was called before the court at Plymouth in June 1650, where Governor Bradford dismissed him with a warning that he and his Separatist believers would have to desist from their meetings. To find religious freedom, Holmes moved to Newport, where he continued his highly skilled trade of glassmaking and became a most active and influential member of Elder Clarke's

Baptist church.

Clarke joined Williams in the long and bitter verbal battle with John Cotton of Boston, Calvinist Puritan leader of Massachusetts. Through speeches, sermons, and printed pamphlets the controversy raged. Williams and Clarke insisted upon the principle that civil magistrates had no authority over the souls of men; Cotton maintained that the authority of the civil officer included control over religious beliefs and practices. He was determined to have a theocratic state.

A Well-Publicized Whipping

Cotton was in a position to enforce his doctrine in the Massachusetts colony, as Clarke learned when he went up to Lynn, near Boston, to visit an aged and blind Baptist friend, William Witter. He was accompanied by Obadiah Holmes and an active layman of his congregation, John Crandall. The men walked the eighty miles' distance in two days and arrived at Witter's home on Saturday night.

Boston authorities were informed that the three dissenters had entered the Massachusetts jurisdiction, and they sent marshals to watch their movements. The Baptist visitors decided to stay with their blind friend overnight and comfort him with a private religious service in his home on Sunday morning.

Suspecting that this was what the three were up to, a marshal and his deputies burst into the blind man's home next morning and caught them in the act of worship. Here was a serious offense, for it was strictly a violation of the law for anyone to hold divine services except under the auspices or with the consent of the established Congregational Church of the Massachusetts Bay Colony. The three culprits were hustled off to a tavern. Then, informed that they would have to cleanse their souls for their disobedience in the matter of worship, they were taken to the afternoon worship in the established church.

Lodged in the Boston jail, the men faced an official charge containing the accusation that they were "certain erroneous persons, being strangers," though actually their offense was understood to be holding a religious meeting without license from the authorities.

Determined to make an example of these somewhat prominent invaders from Rhode Island, the officials staged a well-publicized trial. John Cotton was invited to state the case against these Rhode Island heretics, and he swept grandly into the courtroom to carry out his mission. Sitting in the prisoners' box, Clarke, Holmes, and Crandall heard Cotton shout that the culprits denied the saving power of infant baptism, and thus they were soul-murderers. This offense, declared Cotton with all his fervor, deserved capital punishment just as did any other type of murder.

For their defense, all three affirmed the fact that they were holding a religious service, with reading from the Scripture to their blind friend, and prayers. However, Clarke further pled, it was not a public service; a home should not be invaded by civil authorities, under the ancient English maxim that a man's house, however humble, is his castle.

"Not when a crime is being committed!" John Cotton countered.

The trial judge agreed with the eloquent and learned defender of the established faith. These men, he said, deserved to be put to death. However, he would let them off with a fine. And if they did not pay the fine and leave at once the territory of the colony, they should be "well whipped." So back they went to the jail.

Friends in Newport promptly raised the money for the

fines of all three men. Crandall was released from the fine. John Clarke and Obadiah Holmes refused permission for their fines to be paid. As Clarke was being led to the whipping post, a friend pressed the money into the hands of the Puritan official accompanying the party, and Clarke was released. But Holmes remained adamant.

"Agreeing to the payment of my fine would constitute admission of wrong-doing," he stubbornly maintained.

The streets of Boston from the jail to the public whipping post were lined with spectators. Some raised their voices above the jeering to bid this dissenting preacher to be of good courage. As he was being stripped to the waist, Holmes preached a brief sermon to the dense crowd of men, women, and children that formed a circle about the whipping post, exhorting them to remain faithful to their beliefs.

The whipper took seriously the sentence the judge had pronounced, that his victim be well whipped. According to Holmes's own account, the flogger used a whip with three hard-leather lashes, stopping three times to spit on his hands and laying on with all his might. Each of the thirty strokes cut three gashes through the skin. Holmes recorded that a holy strength and serenity possessed and sustained him through the ordeal. Several voices were heard encouraging and praising him despite the stern looks and hostile gestures of the civil officers present. In Holmes's account is this passage:

"And as the man began to lay the strokes upon my back, I said to the people, though my flesh should fail and my spirit should fail, yet God will not fail: so it pleased the Lord to come in, and to fill my heart and tongue as a vessel full, and with an audible voice I break forth, praying the Lord not to lay this sin to their charge, and telling the people I found he did not fail me, and therefore now I should trust him forever who failed me not; for in truth, as the strokes fell upon me, I had such a spiritual manifestation of God's presence, as I never had before, and the outward pain was so removed from me, that I could well bear it, yea, and in a manner felt it not, although it was grievous." [2]

As soon as Holmes, dripping with blood, was untied, two men rushed up to shake his hand. They were promptly arrested and taken from the crowd to the jail, although, Holmes recorded, all they said was "God bless you!"

John Clarke welcomed back to the peace and freedom of Newport his scarred associate from the Boston jail and whipping post. For twenty days and nights Obadiah Holmes could sleep only by lying on his stomach, or propped upon his knees and elbows. In the meantime news of the trial and the whipping spread far and wide over Massachusetts and Rhode Island communities. The account also reached London, and there Sir Richard Saltonstall asked for full details. He had lived in Boston and had served as magistrate in that city years before. Appalled at the news, he addressed a letter to the ministers of Boston, in which he declared:

"It doth not a little grieve my spirit to hear what sad things are reported daily of your tyranny and persecution in New England; that you fine, whip, and imprison men for their consciences. First, you compel such to come into your assemblies as you know will not join with you in worship, and when they show their dislike thereof, or witness against it, then you stir up your magistrates to punish them for such (as you conceive) their public affronts. Truly, friends, this practice of compelling any in matters of worship to do that whereof they are not fully persuaded, is to make them sin, for so the apostle tells us, Rom. xiv 23. And many are made hypocrites thereby, conforming in their outward man for fear of punishment. We pray for you, and wish your prosperity every way; hoped the Lord would have given you so much love and light there, that you might have been eyes to God's people here, and not to practice those courses in a wilderness, which you went so far to prevent. These rigid ways have laid you very low in the hearts of the saints. I do assure you that I have heard them pray in public assemblies, that the Lord would give you meek and humble spirits, not to strive so much for uniformity as to keep the unity of the spirit in the bond of peace." [3]

That civil authorities could enter a home without a warrant just on the suspicion that a so-called crime by way of religious worship was being committed was a topic of frequent conversation, not only among dissenters, but among other thoughtful citizens as well. The event proved to be an important factor in creating among those rugged pioneers the sentiment to assert the right of all men to be secure in their persons, papers, effects, and homes against unwarranted searches and seizures.

Cromwell Wasn't Interested

By 1651 Elder John Clarke was determined to secure a permanent charter for all the Rhode Island communities, of which Providence, Newport, Warwick, and Portsmouth were now the principal towns. That meant a long, arduous sojourn in London. He left on this mission late in the year only to find that a rugged military genius, Oliver Cromwell, had conquered the forces of King Charles I, had been installed as captain-general of the army and was fast becoming the dictator of the British realm.

The Baptist minister, now returned to his native city of London, supposed the Protestant man at the head of the military and civil regime, with the title of Protector of the Commonwealth, would be sympathetic to the cause of reli-

gious liberty and would speedily grant the request for a
Rhode Island charter. After all, were not the Baptists of
Great Britain solidly behind Cromwell, hoping for a greater
measure of religious freedom from his own hand?

But disappointment dogged Clarke's steps as he made the
rounds from bureau to bureau in the Protectorate government trying to interest someone in seeing Cromwell in behalf
of the dissenters in that far-away American colony. It is
not known if Oliver Cromwell ever heard of Clarke's petition, or if he did, ever seriously considered granting the
charter. Old Ironsides, as the Protector was called, was quite
taken up with plans to advance the Protestant cause in
Europe, but with little thought for the affairs of the colonies.
His overriding ambition was to push the power and prestige
of Britain to the highest possible level. Furthermore, all
through the years of his rule, Cromwell's orientation was
toward centralized control, with individual freedoms, including religious freedom, subordinate.

Baptists of England, however, flocked to Cromwell's ban-
ner, filled the ranks of his army, supported his leadership,
and profited from his favors. The temper of the times gave
to the English people such Baptist molders of opinion as
John Bunyan, son of a tinker who in Bedford jail wrote
Pilgrim's Progress; and by two other noted writers, who are
identified by many historians as Baptists: John Milton, who
in his blindness produced *Paradise Lost;* and after Restoration, Daniel Defoe, whose pen gave to English literature
Robinson Crusoe.

Clarke's stay in London stretched out to twelve long years.
To support himself he returned to the practice of medicine
among old and new friends in London. At last patience and
persistence won the battle for this Baptist minister and doctor
of medicine. On a September day in 1658 Oliver Cromwell

passed from the scene of power. During the next two years
a restoration of the monarchy was brought about and Charles
II was crowned king. Clarke found it possible to interest
a minister of the Crown, and then Charles himself, in the
matter of a charter for Rhode Island.

In 1663 the coveted document was secured, and John
Clarke returned in triumph to his adopted colony, as had
Roger Williams before him. In ringing words the charter
declared:

"Our royal will and pleasure is, that no person within
said Colony, at any time hereafter, shall be in any wise
molested, punished, disquieted, or called in question for any
differences of opinion in matters of religion, and do not
actually disturb the civil peace of said Colony; but that
all and any persons may, from time to time, and at all times
hereafter, freely and fully have and enjoy his and their own
judgments and consciences in matters of religious concernments throughout the tract of land hereafter mentioned, they
behaving themselves peacefully and quietly, not using this
liberty to licentiousness and profaneness, not to civil injury
or outward disturbance of others, any law, statute or clause
therein contained, usage or custom of this realm to the
contrary thereof in any wise notwithstanding." [4]

To this forthright statement were added these words of
the monarch, later engraved upon the state house in Providence for all future generations of Rhode Island people to
ponder: "It is much on their hearts (if they may be permitted)
to hold a lively experiment that a most flourishing civil state
may stand and best be maintained, and that among our
English subjects, with full liberty in religious concernments."

It is most likely that King Charles had the help of the
learned and determined John Clarke in wording the principal
clauses of the charter. It is almost certain that the sovereign,

thinking upon the unusual request he had just granted, added the postscript, never realizing fully to how great an extent the "lively experiment" in religious liberty in Rhode Island would shape the pattern of the American way of life and government when the people of the colonies brought forth a new nation, as Abraham Lincoln later said, "conceived in liberty and dedicated to the proposition that all men are created equal."

Legalized Intolerance

If all the American colonies had caught the ideal of granting freedom of conscience and worship that was Rhode Island's, the dark pages of persecutions for spiritual beliefs in the new world would not have been written. But twelve decades were to pass before the principle of separation of church and state, cherished and nurtured by the Baptists, became the official policy of the American people. More than a century was required for the people of the new nation to gain complete religious liberty, to embody its guarantee in their Constitution, and build it into the fundamental laws of the states as well.

Much of the intolerance of the colonial period was directed squarely at the stubborn, free-thinking Anabaptists, as they were still called in derision. Their practice of baptizing only those who were mature enough to accept religious beliefs was the principal factor that brought down public condemnation on their heads. In 1644 the General Court of the Massachusetts Bay Colony spelled out the offense of refusing to have babies baptized and prescribed punishments for parents and others who sanctioned such refusal. This step was necessary, it was explained by the civil and religious authorities, for two reasons: To save the souls of the infants from hell-fire in case they should die, and to bring uniformity to the administration of religious affairs.

The law struck full force at all dissenters against the established Puritan Church. The General Assembly of Virginia in 1659 enacted a similar law and made its punishments even more severe by amendments in 1662.

In 1636, when the Massachusetts Bay Colony was only six years old, an institution for higher education was founded at the community of New Towne, near Boston. Two years later a young immigrant minister, John Harvard, passed away, leaving half his fortune and all his library to the school. In honor of this benefactor the institution was named Harvard College. Since Cambridge in England was the seat of a noted university the General Court changed the name of New Towne to Cambridge.

Dr. Henry Dunster, a foremost scholar and teacher in the colony, was elected Harvard's president in 1640. He launched the college on its illustrious career by selecting the best available professors of Latin, Greek, mathematics, and what was known as moral science. He encouraged freedom of study and beliefs—the beginning of academic freedom in the new world.

Doing some free-thinking of his own, Dunster became convinced that these peculiar people, the Baptists, were right on two counts: first, in holding to believer's baptism, rather than to the baptism of infants; second, in pleading for freedom of conscience and for spiritual liberty generally. In 1655 he let it be known publicly that he had embraced the Baptist faith.

The blow fell quickly. The overseers of Harvard College summarily dismissed Henry Dunster from his position as president and professor. He moved to Plymouth colony to live in inactivity and disgrace until his death in 1659.

To understand the attitude of intolerance in religious

beliefs and practices prevalent in the seventeenth and eighteenth centuries in the American colonies one must place himself in the setting of that day. The spiritual leaders of the established churches were not more cruel, more sadistic, more prompted by evil motives, than those of other areas of Christendom. They merely lived at a time when state-supported religion was the traditional and accepted thing, backed by the power of the civil authorities.

In New England, the Puritans, and then the Congregationalists, made up the Establishment, tolerating the Episcopalians but not the Anabaptists or any other "separated" faiths. As the other colonies developed, most of them officially recognized and favored some establishment of religion. In Virginia the transplanted Church of England was by law the only recognized church and continued so through the Revolution and the adoption of the United States Constitution, as we have seen in the account of John Leland and his influence upon James Madison in the drafting of the Bill of Rights.

A few colonial areas offered toleration for Baptists and other dissenters. The General Assembly of Maryland, for example, in 1649 passed a much-heralded Act of Toleration. It was hailed as granting religious liberty. Actually, by its own words, the act allowed religious freedom only to those "professing to believe in Jesus Christ . . . and to those who believe God's holy and true Christian religion." The Maryland act further provided:

"That whatsoever person or persons within this Province and the Islands thereunto belonging shall from hence forth blaspheame God, that is, curse him or deny our Saviour Jesus Christ to bee the sonne of God, or shall deny the holy Trinity the father sonne and holy Ghost, or the Godhead of any of the said three persons of the Trinity or the Unity of the Godhead, or shall use or utter any reproachfull speeches words or language concerning the said Holy Trinity, or any of the said three persons thereof shal be punished with death and confiscacon or forfeiture of all his or her lands and goods to the Lord Proprietary and his heires." [5]

One can well understand that this legislation by Maryland failed to satisfy the demands for religious liberty on the part of such sects as the Baptists and the Quakers, to say nothing of that small and despised group, the Jews.

Law Based on the Commandments

It must be remembered that under a legally favored religion, supported by taxation, the civil authorities had a job to do. They were entrusted with making and keeping the people good by law.

Much of the civil law of that day was based upon the Ten Commandments. If the Decalogue required keeping the sabbath day holy, then it was the duty of the civil officers to see to it that violations of keeping the sabbath holy were punished—according to their own interpretation of what constituted the sabbath day, and also of what was holy. John Cotton spelled out the principle:

"And therefore it cannot be truly said the Lord Jesus never appointed the civil sword for a remedy in such case; for he did expressly appoint it in the New Testament; nor did he ever abrogate it in the New; the reason of the law, which is the life of the law, is an eternal force and equity in all ages. 'Thou shalt surely kill him, because he hath sought to thrust thee away from the Lord thy God.' Deut. 13:9–10. This reason is of moral; that is, of universal and perpetual equity, to put to death any apostate seducing idolater or heretick, who seeketh to thrust away the souls of God's people from the Lord their God." [6]

Ministers and parishioners of the established churches in the American colonies, as in their mother countries, permitted no freedom to question the authorized interpretation of the Bible. The medieval concepts of heaven and hell had not been softened and blurred. At every point of time in his life, from birth to death, a person was destined for one place or another—for heaven or for hell.

To understand further the actions of the leaders of the established churches and their champions, the civil authorities, it is essential to keep in mind that to them truth was doctrine as they saw it, and error was a belief that differed from theirs. If baptism was essential to save the soul of an infant from damnation, then infant baptism it must be, and cursed be anyone who stood in the way, whether parent or pastor. The attitude was tersely expressed by the noted Boston preacher, Increase Mather, in a sermon of May 23, 1677, in which he declared:

"I believe that anti-Christ hath not at this day a more probable way to advance his kingdom of darkness, than by a toleration of all religions and persuasions." [7]

It was against this very premise of the established churches that Baptist faith and practice held firm. The Baptists could find no Scripture to support the doctrine of infant damnation or of infant baptism for the salvation of the infant's soul. Not even the strongest Calvinist Baptist could believe that an ordinance administered without the knowledge and free acceptance of the individual could bring about a regeneration of the soul. So the persecutions continued, and suffering for the cause of religious freedom became the badge of honor for Baptist ministers and congregations.

4

WILLIAM SCREVEN
The Baptist Who Planted a Free Church in Warm, Rich Soil

Two significant results flowed from the restrictions and persecutions of early American Baptists:

First, they scattered the seeds of Baptist faith and practice widely over the developing colonies. Second, they crystallized in the minds and hearts of Baptists, as well as others who were of like opinions, the determination to work for guarantees of complete religious liberty—the guarantees that became the foundations of all freedoms in the American nation.

By the year 1677, the Baptists in Boston had grown to a sizeable congregation, meeting quietly in the homes of the faithful. They organized themselves into a church, and in January, 1678, they began building a meeting house without informing the authorities that it was to be used for worship. On February 15, 1679, the congregation met for the first time in the new building. John Russell, a well-educated man, was ordained the first pastor.

By this time, of course, the fact that a Baptist church had been established in Massachusetts' capital city had become well known. At the meeting of the General Court in May an act was passed authorizing the officials of the city to confiscate the Baptist property. The spirited pastor and his congregation moved into the hearing room of the Court, where Elder Russell contended that the act was unjust, since it was passed after the church was built. The law made a crime of something that was not declared a crime before the deed was done. It was, the pastor contended, *ex post facto,* and therefore not justified.

After heated discussion the court voted that the congregation could still own the property, but "it is our judgment that you who are Baptists shall not meet in it again."

Charles II Interfered

Word of this matter reached His Majesty, King Charles II, who did a most unusual thing. He dictated a personal letter, written in his secretary's hand, to the governor and authorities of the Massachusetts Bay Colony. It contained these severe words:

"We shall henceforth expect that there shall be suitable obedience in respect of freedom and liberty of conscience, so as those that desire to serve God in the way of the ch. of Eng, be not thereby made obnoxious or discountenanced from sharing in the government, much less that of any other of our good subjects (not being Papists), who do not agree in the Congregational way, be by law subjected to fines or forfeitures, or other incapacities, for the same; which is a severity to be the more wondered at, whereas liberty of conscience was made a principal motive for your first transportation into those parts." [1]

The Boston authorities decided not to permit the Baptists to know about this royal letter, but the news of it could not be long suppressed. Defiantly, the congregation opened the doors of their meeting house again and resumed services. In March, 1680, the General Court ordered the constables to nail shut the doors once more, and a new act with the threat of severe punishments forbade the Baptists to worship there again.

Once more Pastor Russell and Baptist leaders pled that the *ex post facto* action was contrary to simple justice. But to no avail. The doors of the First Baptist Church of Boston were not reopened until 1689, when the Act of Toleration was signed by King William III in behalf of himself and his royal companion, Queen Mary. This act gave the greatest measure of religious liberty to dissenters of Great Britain that they had enjoyed to that day, and its influence for religious freedom was felt throughout the American colonies.

William Screven Goes South

An early example of the expansion of Baptist churches and their influence is found in the story of Elder William Screven and his congregation. To find religious liberty they journeyed all the way from the northernmost colony, Maine, to the settlement farthest south at that time—South Carolina.

Screven was born in Somerton, England, in 1629, and emigrated to Boston about the year 1668. He became a successful merchant of the city. Deeply religious, he planned to organize a dissenters' church in Boston. Informed that he would be violating the laws of the Massachusetts Bay Colony, he moved to Kittery in the province of Maine. When Massachusetts acquired the area of Maine, Screven joined with several others in petitioning the king to establish direct rule over the province. While this step was never taken, the petition placed William Screven's name on the list of those who might entertain dangerous heresies.

Authorities watched him closely, and on July 6, 1675, they lodged a charge against him, misspelling his name, which read: "We'll present William Scrivine for not frequenting the public meeting according to Law on the Lord's Day." Before the case came to trial the court issued a clearance, stating: "This person presented is remitted because per evidence it appears that he usually attends Mr. Mowdy's meeting on the Lord's day." The Mowdy referred to was Elder Joshua Moody, a Congregationalist minister in Portsmouth.

Screven married Bridget Cutts, daughter of a sea captain who had immigrated from Barbados. To become full-fledged Baptists, in July, 1681, Screven and his wife, with Humphrey Churchwood, a young man of Kittery who later married Bridget's sister Mary, went to Boston and were baptized into the membership of the First Baptist Church. Several of their neighbors who were dissenters also wanted baptism so that they might have their own Baptist congregation. Accordingly, Screven went again to the Boston church and asked that he be licensed to preach and to baptize. A certificate from the church, dated January 11, 1682, and signed by the pastor, Isaac Hull, and Deacon John Farnum, reads:

"These are to certify, that our beloved brother, William Screven, is a member in communion with us, and having had trial of his gifts among us, and finding him to be a man whom God hath qualified and furnished with the gifts of his Holy Spirit, and grace, enabling him to open and apply the word of God, which through the blessing of the Lord Jesus may be useful in his hand, for the begetting and building up of souls in the knowledge of God, do therefore appoint, approve and encourage him, to exercise his gift in the place where he lives, or elsewhere, as the providence of God may cast him: and so the Lord help him to eye his glory in all things, and to walk humbly in the fear of his name."

Now the battle against this dissenter by Kittery religious

and civil authorities began in earnest. Before Screven and his friends could form their congregation they were called before a magistrate, who threatened them with fines and imprisonment if they proceeded with heretical worship or even attended Baptist meetings. On June 28, 1682, Screven was brought by a marshal before the entire General Assembly of the Province of Maine convening at York, and charged with blasphemy in that he "spoke against the holy ordinance of Baptism." He promised (at least the record so states) either to stop holding public services, or to leave the colony.

But in a spirit of defiance, or prompted by a stubborn belief that his cause was just, William Screven made no immediate move to leave Kittery. In September he wrote to the Boston Baptist church and asked for an elder to come to help organize the Baptists into a congregation. Later that month the church was organized, with a covenant signed by William Screven as elder. By his name was that of his wife, Bridget. Signing also were Humphrey Churchwood with his wife, Mary, and eight other men, most of them adding the names of their wives.

When officials of Kittery made known their intention to deal harshly with Screven and his congregation if they tried to hold church services, the preacher finally decided he had had enough of persecutions for conscience's sake. Several of the relatives of the Cutts family had chosen to settle in the Carolinas rather than in the far-northern province of Maine. Bridget and Mary declared that reports from their kin in the southern colony proved there was religious toleration there. Packing as much of their belongings as they could carry, most of the Kittery Baptist families took ship for the Carolinas. The year was 1696.

As far back as 1521 the Spaniards had explored the inlets and bays of the pleasant Carolina region, laying claim to the land in the name of the sovereign of imperial Spain. They had also established several forts, together with their Catholic mission stations to convert the heathen Indians, along the Atlantic coast from Florida to the southern border of Virginia.

Ignoring the claim of the Spaniards, King Charles II in 1663 by a royal grant chartered the Carolina colony to eight noblemen whom he designated as the Lords Proprietors. The grant covered a vast territory in that southernmost British claim in the North American continent, embracing what became the states of North and South Carolina, Tennessee, Georgia, parts of Alabama and Mississippi, and northern Florida. Among the proprietors were Sir Anthony Ashley Cooper and Sir John Colleton. The name Carolina honored both kings, the beheaded Charles I and the sovereign of the restored monarchy, the grantor himself, Charles II.

The First Southern Baptist Church

French Protestant believers, the Huguenots, led by Captain Jean Ribault, had made an attempt in 1562 at colonizing the region that became South Carolina, but they had been chased away by Spanish soldiers and freebooters. The first permanent settlement came in 1670 when a band of hardy English, commissioned by the Lords Proprietors, landed at Albermarle Point and there began to build Charles Town. Soon a group of dissenters arrived, under leadership of Joseph Blake, from Screven's native community, Somersetshire in England. More immigrants, including several of the Cutts family relatives, came from Barbados. Settlers in greater numbers came from England, and in every group there were dissenters who joined the Baptist ranks.

In 1672 a new town site was laid out by the men of Charles Town at Oyster Point, a wedge of land between the Cooper and Ashley rivers, where, as loyal Charlestonians declare, these two rivers join to form the Atlantic Ocean. New business houses and residences were built, and almost the whole community moved into them.

Meanwhile, the colony in South Carolina was constantly harassed by the Spanish, who claimed all the coastal area from Florida northward to the Virginia grant. By land and sea the Spaniards would come, destroying, burning, capturing as many hostages as they could for slave labor at their St. Augustine fort and other Florida strongholds. Hostile Indians and pirates also scourged the Carolinas. But the land was fertile, the climate pleasant; oysters, fish and game were plentiful; and other resources for survival and growth abundant.

About 1696 Elder Screven moved with the congregation from their rural homes into Charles Town, where they took the name "First Baptist Church." The records show that in 1698 Elder Screven purchased land to add to his 1500 acres, and that another grant, in 1700, brought the holdings of this energetic parson to 2600 acres.

For a time, the members of this First Baptist Church in the southern colonies held services in the home of William Chapman. On July 18, 1699, William Elliot, one of the congregation, gave to his fellow Baptists "Lot No. 62 on Church Street," with a statement which declared:

"As well for and in consideration of the brotherly love which he hath for, and doth bear unto the people of the Church of Christ, baptized on profession of faith, distinguished from all others by the name of Anti-paedobaptists, of which Church he professeth himself a member, as to promote and encourage so good and pious a work as the building a place for the said people to meet and worship. . . ."

A meeting house, forty-seven by thirty-seven feet, was completed in late 1700. Screven continued to serve as pastor until about 1708, when the minutes of the church show that the membership had grown to ninety. In a letter to the members, Elder Screven wrote:

"My dear brethren and sisters (for whom God hath made me, poor unworthy me, an instrument of gathering and settling in the faith and order of the gospel), my request is that you as speedily as possible supply yourselves with an able and faithful minister. Be sure you take care the person be orthodox in the faith, and of blameless life, and does own the Confession put forth by our brethren in London."

Screven's labors ended on October 10, 1713. A tribute to his effective leadership was unwittingly given by a representative of the Anglican Bishop of London who was in Charles Town at the time, when he characterized Screven as "extremely ignorant," but added: "Next to the Presbyterians, the Anabaptists are most numerous."

In all the American colonies, as the new century began, the seeds of Baptist faith and practice had been planted which were to make these peculiar and indomitable people the most numerous of the United States Protestants.

The Welsh and the Tunkers

As the year 1700 dawned, there were only fourteen Baptist churches in the American colonies from Maine to South Carolina. But the new century brought a stirring of interest in religion for the pioneers, and no group benefited more than did the Baptists.

In William Penn's Sylvan Land dissenters found a climate of toleration, and Baptist congregations took root. In 1688 several Welsh immigrants joined settlers from Rhode Island to organize a church in their community. It was the first Baptist church in Pennsylvania, and still exists as Lower Dublin Baptist Church. Members of this congregation proudly announced there would be "preaching or exhorting" every Sunday, and two meetings a year especially to transact the business of the church. Their greatest missionary contribution was to help the Philadelphia Baptists to organize their own first church in 1698.

By 1707 there were five Baptist churches in the Philadelphia area. Inspired by the desire to aid one another in every way possible, the pastors and members of these five churches organized the Philadelphia Baptist Association. Each church sent messengers, with strict instructions that they could not bind their churches to any agreement, since the autonomy of a Baptist church had to be preserved. The messengers could confer, consult, and discuss matters pertaining to doctrine, ordinances, discipline of members, and such like, and report back to their parent churches "for consideration and edification."

Here was the beginning of a significant influence in Baptist life, the *association of churches,* first on the local level, expanding later into *conventions* of messengers representing the churches of entire states and the nation. Here was the tool that shaped the structure of common activities among Baptists and that still surmounts differences in doctrinal matters and creates unity in methods and programs.

In 1719 there came the first shiploads of so-called "Tunkers" from Germany. Also known as Dunkards, they were direct descendants of the Anabaptists in their country. Among them was Elder Paul Palmer, a General Baptist who moved from Maryland to North Carolina in 1727 and established the first Baptist church in that state near the settlement of Cisco. An enthusiastic, vigorous evangelist,

Palmer held numerous revival meetings and organized several churches in various communities of the North Carolina colony. On October 12, 1729, Royal Governor Richard Everard protested to his London bishop: "This Baptist preacher is stirring up a tide of fervor with his wild preaching and exhorting."

The records do not disclose what, if any, action was taken by either His Grace the London Bishop, or His Excellency the Royal Governor.

Morgan Edwards, a noted Baptist historian of the pre-Revolutionary period who lived in Philadelphia, in 1772 issued in his own handwriting a book called *Materials Towards a History of the Baptists in the Provinces of Maryland, Virginia, North Carolina, South Carolina, and Georgia.* A careful writer of names, places, dates, and other details of Baptist life in the southern states, Edwards tells of the founding of churches, persecutions of ministers and their congregations, the disputes between Particular and General Baptists. He begins his account of the spread of Baptist faith to Virginia by remarking:

"Next to Maryland, towards the south, is Virginia; a province famous for tobacco, and antiquity; being the first of all the British provinces in America, and affording much gratification to snuffers, smokers, and chewers in all the rest and in other parts of the world. This weed makes the planters and manufacturers rich and swells the public revenue but must fail, as the raising of it hath already made a barren waste of a great part of the country." [2]

Following this blast at Virginia's principal crop in that pre-Revolutionary day, the learned Baptist writer confirmed that progress for the Baptists was painful and slow for many years due to the fact that the charter granted to the Virginia founders in 1607 officially established the Anglican Church, supported from public funds to the extent necessary to maintain the meeting places and pay the salaries of the rectors. However, Dr. Morgan Edwards added, the Baptists had a way of "persevering to the end," even though it was not until 1714 that the first Anabaptist church was organized in Virginia, in the wilderness of Prince George's County.

The Great Awakening

By the 1720's the established churches in both the American colonies and in the British Isles had for the most part become so established as to be rigid. Their worship services were formal, with little warmth and feeling. Few churches in America offered their worshipers the experience that those peculiar people, the Baptists, called heartfelt religion. The result was a steady decline in church attendance and interest in spiritual matters. The times demanded a revival of religious feeling.

The revival came, on both sides of the Atlantic, in what became known as the Great Awakening. Its first trumpet notes to arouse the people from their spiritual lethargy were blown by a father-and-son team of Presbyterian ministers, William and Gilbert Tennent: by Theodore J. Frelinghuysen of New Jersey, and by Oliver Hart of Pennsylvania, an earnest Baptist who came as a missionary to the Carolinas.

William Tennent lived in a community north of Philadelphia, where he had set up an academy called the Log College, a precise description of the rude building that housed it. Gilbert Tennent studied for the ministry in his father's Log College and became pastor of the New Brunswick, New Jersey, Presbyterian Church in 1726. Two years later he bagan a revival service in his church with remarkable success. Young Tennent preached a fiery, heart-stirring sermon, and people crowded in to hear him. Assisted by his father, Gilbert carried his evangelistic crusade to many communities of New Jersey and Pennsylvania.

Like the Tennents, other outstanding leaders of the Great Awakening in America were not Baptists. Yet the Baptists became the principal beneficiaries of this spiritual movement, since it spread far, wide, and deeply an acceptance of the Baptist ideal of heartfelt religion.

In New England there was Jonathan Edwards, Connecticut-born minister of a Congregational church in Massachusetts. As a child Jonathan was precocious, writing learned essays on religion and philosophy in his early teens and graduating from Yale College with high honors at the age of seventeen. At twenty-four he was called to be pastor at Northampton, a church which his maternal grandfather, the Rev. Solomon Stoddard, had served.

A magnetic speaker, Jonathan Edwards delivered his sermons with an almost fanatical conviction that every word he said was gospel truth and would be disbelieved at the peril of his hearers. Hundreds were added to the membership of Edwards' church, and his influence spread to many other communities.

At the same time a stirring of religious emotion began in England and Wales. Foremost leader of the movement in England was George Whitefield, a preacher of tremendous power and a New Light Congregationalist who believed that the souls of men could best be quickened by an emotional experience resulting in a changed life.

At the urging of John Wesley, Whitefield arrived in Savannah in May, 1738, and preached for three months in all the communities along the coast and in the neighboring islands. Returning to England, he found that the clergy of his homeland had turned against him because of his unorthodox evangelizing, so he took to preaching in the open air to such crowds as never before in England had come to hear a minister. He came back to America in 1740 and in the following decade made five additional journeys to preach to throngs of American people who assembled to hear him from Maine to Georgia. From every congregation, whether in churches or in the open air, men and women moved forward at his invitation to touch him or to press his hand and to ask for his prayers for their salvation.

Numerous converts of this revival period trooped into Baptist congregations, seeking freedom from the established churches. Many became Baptist preachers and founded their own free congregations. Typical of these was John Clayton, an immigrant to the Georgia colony. A forthright exhorter given to speaking his mind, Parson Clayton declared in a sermon: "No man can be a Christian who keeps a concubine, be the keeper a king and the concubine a countess!" [3]

Although Clayton had called no names, his remark was taken as a reflection, as indeed the preacher intended it to be, upon the honor of the late King George I, who had as one of his mistresses a lady of royal blood. For this offense, the indiscreet preacher was arrested and brought before the magistrate at Savannah. In answer to the accusation Clayton made this plea: "I expressed only my private opinion, and I should have the right to do so because I spoke what I considered to be the truth!"

This did not help him much. The magistrate levied a fine upon the parson. Yet without realizing the importance of his protests, Elder Clayton of colonial Georgia was expressing an ideal strenuously defended by Baptists in later years. They called it *Freedom of Speech.*

5

ISAAC BACKUS
The Baptist Who Lobbied
for Religious Freedom Against John Adams

James Lane, who had owned a farm near the town of Richmond, Virginia, from the early years of the eighteenth century, had a son Dutton who disobeyed his explicit orders not to go hear that fiery evangelist, George Whitefield, preach. Not only did Dutton Lane go to hear Whitefield, but under the spell of the great preacher's magnetic voice, personality, and ardor, the youth made a profession of faith. While Dutton Lane knew that Whitefield was an English Separatist and not a Baptist, he liked what Whitefield preached about religious freedom. So Lane joined a small Baptist church there in the heart of Virginia, was ordained to preach, and began his own remarkable career as an evangelist.

Mary Lane Had a Will

This disobedience and drift into heresy so enraged James Lane that he disowned his son and warned his wife never to go hear Dutton preach. However, she was a strong-willed woman. At the time when the promise to obey in the marriage ceremony was taken literally by wives and strictly enforced by husbands, Mary Lane did what she thought was right, with or without her husband's consent. So, on a Sunday morning when Dutton came to hold what was known as a protracted meeting in the Baptist church nearest the Lane plantation, Mary slipped out of the house, put the sidesaddle on her mare, and went to hear him.

Mary Lane readily admitted to her husband that she had gone to the Baptist meeting house to hear their son preach. Seizing his horsewhip, James Lane stood his wife against the wall and beat her unmercifully. Then he took his musket, loaded it with powder and ball, vowed to heaven he would find his heretic son and kill him, and rode away.

For some reason, probably the sight of Lane's musket and his obvious anger, no one around the vicinity of the Baptist meeting house seemed to know where the young preacher had gone. The father returned home, somewhat cooled off by his ride. There the spirited Mary, still nursing the wounds from her husband's whip, quietly challenged his sporting blood: "You give a bird a chance to wing afore you shoot it," she said, "Why not give Dutton a chance? Go hear him just once."

After some hesitation, James Lane agreed. He would go hear his son—just this once. When the service was over, Lane shook his son's hand and walked out without a word. But he came back—time and again, and sat as under a spell while his son called people to repentance and salvation through faith in Jesus Christ. In relating what happened, many times in his career as a pastor and evangelist, Elder Dutton Lane would say: "At last he decided I was preaching the truth. He came forward under conviction of sin. I baptized him, and he became a pillar of that church!" [1]

Lane's power as an eloquent preacher and powerful evangelist became known all over Virginia. Morgan Edwards, eighteenth-century Baptist historian, had this to say about one of Lane's converts: "William Cocker had conceived such a malignity against the Baptists that he was wont to say He had rather go to hell than to heaven if going to the latter required his being a Baptist; but coming accidentally to hear Dutton Lane this same malignant fell to the ground, roaring, 'Lord, have mercy on me! I am a gone man. What shall I do to be saved?' In this manner he went on for about an hour; and now is a humble and pious Baptist."

Salvation for the Common People

Parson Dutton Lane was one of hundreds of Baptists of the mid-1700s who professed religion and answered the call to preach in the period of the Great Awakening. More definitely than they could ever have known, the leaders of the revival movement, whether Baptists or not, paved the way for Baptist growth in America. They followed the example of Whitefield in proclaiming: "Salvation is yours for the taking! Think for yourselves. The common people heard Jesus gladly. You are the common people—you can hear and heed him, too!"

Since Baptists generally were indeed of the common people, they gained a major share of the converts who listened to the trumpet call to salvation and church membership.

There was the Rev. Robert Feke of Oyster Bay, New York, for example, who in 1741 organized a Baptist church there, the first congregation of Baptists in that state. Elder Feke wrote to his friends in Newport who had encouraged his efforts: "God has begun a glorious work among us, and I hope he will carry it on to his own glory, and the salvation of many souls. There have been seventeen added to our little band in about three months." [2]

The Baptist pastor's hope was amply justified as many New England settlers came westward and founded Baptist

churches along the Mohawk, Susquehanna, and Genesee
rivers, and by Otsego Lake. In 1762 the first Baptist church
in New York City was formed with the Rev. John Gano
as pastor. After a distinguished career in the city, Elder
Gano journeyed to the wilds of Kentucky to take the Baptist
message to the West.

Another lasting influence of the revival period in the
American colonies was increased resistance of Baptists, aided
by other dissenters, to laws they considered unjust and intol-
erable, laws sponsored by established churches to govern
religious affairs. In 1718 the General Court of Massachusetts
had put on the books an act that assessed all the families
of the towns in the colony for the payment of salaries of
the Congregational ministers, regardless of whether the families were Presbyterians, Quakers, Baptists, or of any other
faith, or of no faith at all. The tax was levied upon everyone,
"assessed in the king's name," as the General Court declared.

At Swansea, settled by Baptists as a small colony, there
were two Baptist churches and none other. Here the pastors
and congregations refused to pay the tax to support a Congregational minister living in another town serving not one
single family in Swansea. "Taxation without representation,
and without benefit of any public service!" the Baptist
faithful cried.

After appeals and threats failed to convince these stubborn
people that they had to pay the assessment, the authorities
put the property of the Baptist congregations up for sheriff's
sale. The buildings and their furnishings, together with several fields and even a cemetery, were sold for a fraction
of their money value. The Congregational minister himself
was a successful bidder for one parcel.

"Taxation without representation!" the Massachusetts
Baptists cried, anticipating the slogan that was to be raised

three decades later against the tax collectors of Great Britain.

In Virginia, the Act of Toleration, passed in 1689, proved an empty gesture for religious dissenters. It still required a license from the authorities at Williamsburg to hold services, but in Camden County in 1743 a convert of George Whitefield's preaching, Samuel Morris, defied the authorities and invited his neighbors to come to his home for Baptist worship. By some fortune Morris secured a book of sermons preached by Whitefield and taken down after a fashion of shorthand. To an evergrowing group of his neighbors, hungry for any evangelistic sermon and especially one "writ down" from the great English preacher, Morris read and re-read the burning words of the evangelist.

Before long the zealous, literate convert was traveling all over Hanover County to read to groups of listeners at night. The next move was to start building a meeting house. Now the authorities stepped in. A warrant was issued, calling Samuel Morris before the magistrate, where he was charged with "nonattendance at church."

Morris pled that the Act of Toleration applied to Virginia, as to all other of His Majesty's colonies in America, and that thus it applied to him and to his fellow Baptists. The magistrate did not agree, but let Elder Morris off with a stiff warning. After a period of quietude the Baptist missionary-evangelist again took up his preaching and completed the building of a meeting house for his congregation.

Isaac Backus Made Two Decisions

For Baptists of colonial America the most important product of the aroused spiritual movement was Isaac Backus. As a youth just come of age, he went forward to shake Whitefield's hand one night in the spring of 1743 in the Congregational church house at Norwich, Connecticut.

Isaac's late father, Samuel Backus, had passed away six years before, leaving a comfortable fortune made from his iron works and a large estate of land. Samuel Backus was a descendant of one of the first families of Connecticut. Isaac's mother, Elizabeth Tracy Backus, was from the Winslow family of the Mayflower pilgrims.

The Backus family had always been prosperous, but unlike most prosperous people of that day they were independent in religious thinking. Both Isaac's grandfather and great-grandfather had withdrawn from the state-supported Congregational Church in protest against lack of religious freedom in the combination of civil and spiritual rule exercised by the established church. Isaac's mother, however, had remained in the Congregational Church, and at eighteen Isaac himself had joined this favored fellowship in Norwich. It had seemed the proper thing to do.

By a covenant officially approved by the General Court of the Massachusetts Bay Colony in 1657, the Congregational establishment admitted to membership persons who professed to be only moral but not converted, and who agreed to come under the discipline of the church. Both Widow Backus and her son were unhappy in a fellowship that did not require what the Congregational dissenters, known as New Lights, called a true inward change. In 1745 Elizabeth Backus and Isaac cut their ties with the regular Congregational Church and joined the New Light worshipers in Norwich.

Within a few months Isaac Backus made another great decision: He would be a preacher. He applied to his church for ordination, was accepted, and in a solemn ceremony was examined and commissioned by the New Light fellowship to preach. Two years later he began his remarkable career as a minister and spiritual leader. He assembled a congregation at Titicut, Massachusetts, drew up its articles of faith, and became the congregation's first pastor.

Young Preacher Backus looked upon John Locke as his hero and often quoted him in his early writings. He was especially impressed with Locke's treatise *On Toleration*, with its significant words: "Civil laws are not to provide for the truth of opinion but for the safety and security of the commonwealth, and of every particular man's goods and person. And so it ought to be, for truth certainly will do well enough if she were once left to shift for herself." [3]

From the start of his ministry Backus refused to pay the church tax. On February 6, 1749, he was clapped in jail for this refusal, and only the intervention of some influential members of his congregation got him out. Still refusing to pay the tax, he was released with a warning that the levy must be paid or he would be confined for a long term.

Unterrified, Backus stepped up his efforts to repeal the church tax, and in late May, 1749, wrote in his diary:

"On May 24, 1749, many of the saints met together in Attelborough; to seek the Lord's direction and to confer about petitioning the court for to set us free from the oppression of being forced to pay for the support of a worship that we can't in conscience join with—and we had considerable clearness in sending and we drew up a petition and sent copys around to the saints in various parts of the governments; and it fell to my lot to carry a copy down to the cape." [4]

The New Light saints at the Cape warmly endorsed the protest, but the members of the General Court were not impressed. They ignored all such petitions, whether from New Lights, Baptists, Presbyterians, or other troublesome minorities. However, Isaac Backus had exercised a right that he vigorously defended all the rest of his life, that of petition for redress of grievances.

Back in Norwich, Widow Backus fared even worse than her son for her stubborn refusal to pay the tax for support of the established church. One chill autumn night the constables came to her home and escorted her to jail. She had only the clothes she had on her back. For thirteen days and nights she was kept in a cheerless, cold cell of the prison until finally a friend paid the tax for her, and she was released. The spirited woman wrote to her son Isaac: "Though the punishment was grievous, I did not fear; for the Lord was with me."

Drawing ever closer to Baptist beliefs and practices, in August, 1751, Isaac Backus had himself immersed in the open waters of a lake near Titicut. Several of his congregation followed his example. He continued in his position as pastor of his church until June, 1756. Then came his open espousal of the Baptist faith.

It is likely that his members were not too surprised. For years Backus had been preaching and defending the ideals for which Baptists were most noted: spiritual liberty, believer's baptism for membership in the church, the autonomy of each church congregation, and complete freedom from governmental control.

The congregation of the First Baptist Church of Middleborough, Massachusetts, called Elder Isaac Backus to be the pastor, and he accepted. There he began the pastorate that extended until his death in 1806.

Backus continued the campaigns he had begun as a New Light Congregationalist against taxation of religious bodies, even though the laws of both Massachusetts and Connecticut had been modified to permit Baptists to avoid paying taxes to support the state-approved church and its ministers, provided they signed certificates of exemption announcing that they were bona fide Baptists. Civil and religious authorities of these colonies considered this a very tolerant arrangement, and most Baptist congregations were signing the certificates, glad to be rid of the unjust tax. But the Rev. Isaac Backus denounced this scheme, holding that to force Baptists to sign the certificates before they could secure tax exemption was as much an invasion of personal rights as the tax itself. He continued to declare that to comply with this law implied that the civil rulers had the right to favor one religious group over another, and that by levying this tax the authorities were appropriating a power that belonged only to God as the spiritual head of all believers. Finally, he condemned the practice because, he said: "In all civil governments some are appointed for others, and have power to compel others to submit to their judgment; but our Lord has most plainly forbidden us, either to assume or submit to any such thing in religion." [5]

Backus realized that the Baptists, drawing their members in largest part from farmers and laboring people with little education, were generally led by ministers of meager schooling. It was a rare thing to find an academy graduate among them. For the future good of the growing sect, Backus decided, this must be remedied. He joined with other well-known Baptist leaders, particularly those in Philadelphia, to establish a college especially for candidates for the Baptist ministry, and in 1766 they founded Rhode Island College at Providence, later to become Brown University. The scholarly James Manning, a Princeton graduate, became its first president. Backus served as a trustee of the school for thirty years, helping to bring high recognition to the institution among early colleges in America. For many years it was the chief training ground and seminary for young Baptist ministers. Proud of its reputation as a Baptist institution, the college refused to consider any plan for state support or control.

By 1762 the Philadelphia Baptist Association had grown to twenty-nine churches with more than four thousand members, chiefly in Pennsylvania, New Jersey, and New York. Following the pattern set by this first cooperating group of Baptist churches, other groups formed themselves into associations for united efforts and mutual benefit. The second such association was made by congregations of the Charleston, South Carolina, area, grouping about the Old First Baptist Church. Next came the Sandy Creek Baptists in North Carolina in 1758 and Ketockton Baptist Association in Virginia in 1766.

The Sandy Creek churches were known as Separate Baptists, and in 1770 they had grown strong enough to divide into three associations, one each in Virginia, North Carolina, and South Carolina. Leader of the Separates in the latter state was Elder Daniel Marshall, a fervent evangelist and organizer of churches. He was arrested by South Carolina authorities at the insistence of Anglican Church leaders for his preaching and pleading the cause of religious liberty. Discussing the influence of those who went out from old Sandy Creek, the contemporary historian, Morgan Edwards, with some pardonable exaggeration declared:

"All the Separate Baptists sprang hence: not only eastward towards the sea, but westward towards the great river Mississippi, but northward to Virginia and southward to South Carolina and Georgia. The word went forth from this sion, and great was the company of them who published it, in so much that her converts were as the drops of morning dew."

The Grievance Committee

Urging that New England Baptists fall in line, in 1767 Elder Backus and Dr. Manning took the lead in establishing the Warren Baptist Association, made up of churches scattered over the wide region of Massachusetts, Connecticut, and Rhode Island, with Warren, Massachusetts, as its center.

The Warren Baptist Association took the unusual step of setting up a grievance committee composed of eight members so that differences of all kinds among the ministers, congregations, and individual members could be explored and settled. Even more important, the organization appointed an agent to be spokesman for the member churches in all matters of public concern and especially in clashes with the authorities over church taxation. The Rev. John Davis, youthful pastor of the Second Baptist Church, Boston, was named agent. He lived only three years after assuming this work, and when Backus was chosen to succeed he wasted no time announcing that he would "give advice and aid to persons who might be oppressed and harassed for refusing to pay taxes to support the ministers and work of the Congregationalists." Within a few months he brought out in printed form an *Appeal to the Publick for Religious Liberty,* which asserted:

"And it appears to us that the true difference and exact limits between ecclesiastical and civil government is this, That the church is armed with *light and truth,* to pull down the strongholds of iniquity, and to gain souls to Christ, and into his Church . . . While the state is armed with the *sword* to guard the peace, and the civil rights of all persons and societies, and to punish those who violate the same . . . I before declared that the Scripture is abundantly clear for a free support of ministers, but not a forced one; and observed, that there is as much difference between them, as there is between the power of truth in the mind, and the power of the sword in the body."

On May 5, 1773, Elder Backus led the Grievance Committee of the Warren Baptist Association to send a letter, signed by himself as their agent, to all the affiliated churches asking them to petition the state and local governments against requiring the signing of certificates for tax exemption. "We desire you to consider whether it is not our duty to refuse any conformity to their laws about such affairs, even so much as giving any certificates to their assessors," the letter urged.

There is no record that the General Court of Massachusetts, or any local authorities, paid any attention to the petitions, but Backus was exemplifying the use of a right he lived to see guaranteed in the federal Constitution.

The clouds of rebellion against the mother country were gathering over the colonies, and under those clouds the First Continental Congress met in 1774. Delegates from all the thirteen colonies except Georgia convened in Philadelphia intent upon discussing the common problems of the uncertain future.

Elder Backus, agent of the Warren Baptist Association, presented the honorable gentlemen another and unwanted problem: what to do about religious liberty. He won support among fellow ministers for a plan to petition the Continental Congress for an end to the use of public funds for any church or religious group. While few of the agent's associates and friends held much hope for the success of the audacious idea, several willingly accompanied him to Philadelphia to see what his arguments and eloquence might accomplish.

John Adams Was Irritated

Massachusetts had originated the call for the Continental Congress, and one of the state's outstanding leaders, John Adams, had helped to draft its wording. Backus knew that Adams' support for his petition would go far to influence the other fifty-four members from the twelve states gathered in that historic session.

The Baptist delegates from Massachusetts arranged for a conference with the representatives from their state to be held the evening of October 14, 1774, in Carpenters Hall. Because of the high interest in the matter of religious freedom in Massachusetts, several members of the Congress from other states were also present when James Manning read the petition, and Backus rose to explain it.

The Massachusetts delegates, led by John Adams, were visibly embarrassed and irritated. They heartily resented any group implying that their great state did not grant all the religious freedom allowed in all others. Mr. Adams spoke, followed by Samuel Adams, both of them admitting that there was what they called an ecclesiastical establishment but protesting that it was "very slender" and that it permitted full religious freedom. If there were any restrictions on religious liberty in Massachusetts, John Adams declared, it was the fault of local officials who might not understand the law, rather than the General Court.

Backus reminded the group that the General Court had seized the Baptist property at Ashfield in payment of taxes levied for a Congregational minister who did not even live in that parish, and asserted that it was not so much a matter of the money involved, as one of principle in which freedom of conscience, with freedom also from state control, was at stake.

John Adams closed the four-hour discussion with a promise that the Massachusetts delegates would do what they could for the relief of the Baptists, then, according to Backus, added these words: "Gentlemen, if you mean to try to affect a change in Massachusetts laws respecting religion, you may

as well attempt to change the course of the sun in the
heavens!"

John Hancock Ordered a Reading

Determined to change the course of the sun in the heavens
if necessary, Backus and his committee armed themselves
with another and more strongly worded petition, and presented their plea directly to John Hancock, presiding over
the Continental Congress. Mr. Hancock ordered the petition
read and considered. After some discussion the members took
action. It was expressed in this resolution:

"In Provincial Congress, Cambridge, December 9, 1774:
On reading the memorial of the Rev. Isaac Backus, agent
to the Baptist churches in this government: Resolved, that
the establishment of civil and religious liberty, to each
denomination in the province, is the sincere wish of this
Congress; but being by no means vested with powers of
civil government, whereby they can redress the grievances
of any person whatever, they therefore recommend to the
Baptist churches, that when a general assembly shall be
convened in this colony, they lay the real grievances of said
churches before the same, when and where their petition
will most certainly meet with all that attention due to the
memorial of a denomination of Christians, so well disposed
to the public weal of their country. By order of the Congress,
John Hancock, President." [6]

That suggestion was all that the persistent Backus and
his resolute Baptist associates needed. When the General
Court met at Watertown in July, 1775, early in the session
the members heard and pondered this vigorous memorial
from Baptists of their state:

"Our real grievances are, that we, as well as our fathers,

have from time to time been taxed on religious accounts where we were not represented: and when we have sued for our rights, our causes have been tried by interested judges . . . and for a civil legislature to impose religious taxes, is, we conceive, a power which their constituents never had to give, and is, therefore, going entirely out of their jurisdiction . . . We beseech this honorable Assembly to take these matters into their wise and serious consideration before Him, who has said, *with what measure ye mete, it shall be measured to you again.* Is not all America now appealing to Heaven, against the injustice of being taxed where we are not represented; and against being judged by men, who are interested in getting away our money? Yet as we are persuaded that an entire freedom from being taxed by civil rulers to religious worship, is not a mere favour, from any man or men in the world, but a right and property granted us by God."

The memorial was read twice, discussed, referred to a committee, and reported favorably. A bill was drafted which stated that "no person shall be hurt or restrained, in person, liberty or estate, for worshiping God in the manner most agreeable to the dictates of his conscience." A time was set for its second reading, and Backus and his fellow Baptists were ready to celebrate what they thought would be a significant triumph. But a vote on the bill was postponed from day to day and finally the bill itself was tabled, according to agent-lobbyist Backus, because John Adams had been quietly at work behind the scenes.

Backus was often referred to by his opponents as the most contentious person they ever encountered. Even by his friends he was recognized as one who liked to debate for debate's sake, often with harsh words better left unsaid. To gain a point Backus was known to lead the discussion into several side fields, only to drag his unwary participants in the dialogue into concessions they did not intend to make. Too often for Backus the end justified the verbal means.

At the same time, Backus also learned what it meant to be villified and condemned by those opposing his principles. Every week the newspapers of Massachusetts printed tirades against him, some of the writers calling him a fanatic, others a "treasonable scoundrel." He was accused of going to Philadelphia "to attempt to break up the Union of our Colonies," and one editor asserted: "For this man, the halter and gallows would be fitting reward."

Some of the denunciations Backus answered in his usual stilted prose with its long, involved sentences. Some attacks he ignored as not worthy of answer. Disappointed but still undaunted, he would wait his time to return to the battle.

"We Hold These Truths to Be Self-Evident . . ."

In the meantime, clouds of a greater conflict over human liberties continued ominously to gather. The dispute between the government of His Majesty George III and his American colonies was reaching the point of no return. Open rebellion on the part of American leaders was now the steam which the kettle of political control could no longer restrain.

Patrick Henry, the eloquent Virginia lawyer who had upheld the right of Baptists and other dissenters to worship freely, had asserted the right of the colonial states to legislate independent of the British Parliament, especially with respect to taxation. On April 19, 1775, the first shots of the War for Independence sounded on the village green of Lexington, Massachusetts. The Continental Congress assigned the command of the Continental Army to General George Washington.

On July 2, 1776, the Congress adopted a forthright Declaration of Independence, written by a delegate from Virginia, Thomas Jefferson. Announced to the public two days later, it contained these historic words: "We hold these truths to be self-evident, that all men are created equal, that they are endowed by their Creator with certain unalienable rights, among these Life, Liberty, and the Pursuit of Happiness."

From that time forward, Thomas Jefferson, although not a Baptist, became in the mind of Isaac Backus and of countless other Baptist leaders the ideal statesman.

Buttressed by the Declaration, even before independence was won, all the states except Rhode Island and Connecticut adopted new constitutions. The General Court of Massachusetts called a convention for that purpose in 1779. Noah Alden, a Baptist of Boston, urged Backus to offer the draft of a bill of rights for the new constitution. Noah Alden's letter, preserved among Backus' papers, has a notation on the back which reads: "Wrote a Bill of Rights, and sent in a letter to him. August 11, 1779."

Backus must have had before him a copy of the bill of rights already adopted by Virginia, and possibly also by Pennsylvania, for the wording of his proposal contained phrases almost identical to those in the constitutions of those states. Some words were similar also to those Backus used in his Memorial of 1774. The first article declared: "All men are born free and equal, and have certain natural, essential, and unalienable rights."

A second article asserted that "no subject shall be hurt, molested, or restrained, in his person, liberty, or estate, for worshiping God in the manner and season most agreeable to the dictates of his own conscience."

In Backus' draft was an article that actually prohibited the levying of taxes to support *any* church. Again to his disappointment, this wording was deleted from the final draft of the Massachusetts constitution. Backus vigorously protested this omission in a paper entitled *An Appeal to the People of Massachusetts Against Arbitrary Power*, published in the December 2, 1779, issue of the *Boston Chronicle*. The paper could not affect the wording already adopted. Still, Isaac Backus' ideal of religious liberty was taking root.

6

SUNDRY PATRIOTS
The Baptists Who Proclaimed
Freedom of Soul, Southward and Westward

No church fellowship in America was more hearty in its support of the War for Independence than the Baptists. According to Isaac Backus only two Baptist ministers, whose names he did not mention, refused to support the struggle. The great majority of Baptist ministers, in their sermons and their evangelistic tours, actively announced that they stood with General Washington, the Continental Congress, and the armed forces fighting for freedom from Great Britain.

As the acknowledged leader of colonial Baptists and their chief spokesman for the cause of religious liberty, Backus himself lost no chance to endorse the Revolution. He repeatedly declared that it was the right of the people to establish their own government, especially if it meant greater personal freedoms. Said Backus:

"The great end of government being for the good of the governed and not the honor or profit of any particular person or families therein: the community hath an inalienable right to reform, alter, or newly form their constitution of government, as that community shall judge to be most conducive to the public weal." [1]

It was well known and appreciated by all Baptist leaders

in the colonial states that the Virginia country squire and
statesman, Thomas Jefferson, had supported them and the
leaders of other faiths who were struggling to secure religious
liberty. They rejoiced when he wrote into the Declaration
of Independence the stirring words: "That to secure these
rights, governments are instituted among men, deriving their
just powers from the consent of the governed."

"This is what we have believed and taught all along!"
was the exultant cry of Baptists from New England to Georgia.

Many Baptists went back to the statements of Roger
Williams and found striking similarities in the words of the
Rhode Island founder and those of the Virginia delegate
to the Congress. They wondered if Thomas Jefferson might
have been reading Roger Williams' writings on human liberty. As freedom had been the watchword of Baptists in
matters of conscience and worship, so freedom and self-
government in political affairs became their goal once war
with the mother country was joined.

While Baptist leaders generally supported the obligation
of every able-bodied male citizen to take part in the war
by bearing arms, they also defended the right of any man
who in conscience could not bear arms, "who conscientiously
scruples the lawfulness of it, if he will pay such equivalent,"
as a resolution of the Warren Baptist Association stated it.
This stand brought Baptists to the defense of Quakers and
Mennonites who traditionally were staunch pacifists. Dr.
Backus proudly recorded:

"The Baptists were so generally united with their country
in defense of their privileges, that when the General Court
at Boston passed an act, in October 1778, to debar all men
from returning to their government, whom they judged to
be their enemies, and named 311 men, such there was not

one Baptist among them. Yet there was scarce a Baptist member in the Legislature who passed this act." [2]

Baptist preachers joined those of other denominations—principally Episcopalians, Methodists, and Presbyterians—as voluntary chaplains to the Revolutionary soldiers in all the thirteen states. Where commanders of the troops permitted, these ministers set up rude altars in the camps on Sunday mornings and among the campfires at night. They preached to men dirty with the dust of the march and the bivouac and often wearing bandages red from the wounds of battle, but eager to hear what they used to hear in the churches back home.

In Georgia there was Daniel Marshall, serving as a chaplain to the Southern troops under General Nathanael Greene. Tory sympathizers took him prisoner, but he is reported to have "preached" them into releasing him, whereupon he rejoined the Revolutionary army and marched northward with it against Cornwallis' Redcoats.

Against English Rule and Satan

Elder Oliver Hart, pastor of the First Baptist Church at Charleston, South Carolina, during the first years of the war preached independence for South Carolina and the other American states as vigorously as he did the gospel. It was said of him that Parson Hart never made any distinction between freedom from English rule and freedom from the rule of Satan. This preacher helped to organize all the coastal areas of South Carolina to supply equipment, clothing, and food for the American troops. He frequently visited the camps of the buckskin-clad Carolina marksmen fighting under the commands of General Francis (Swamp Fox) Marion and General Nathanael Greene, and other units of the American line, with boxes and bales of supplies as they drove the British steadily back toward Virginia. Such activities marked Parson Hart as a traitor in the eyes of the British, and when the Redcoats captured Charleston in 1780 the patriotic preacher fled to Hopewell, New Jersey. There he served as pastor of the Baptist congregation until his death in 1795.

When on October 19, 1781, General Charles Cornwallis, British commander, surrendered his troops to the victorious alliance of American and French forces under General Washington and General Rochambeau at Yorktown, Virginia, members of the Philadelphia Baptist Association were meeting in their Triennial Convention. The historic news was carried northward by riders on fast horses and reached Philadelphia near midnight of the next day. In the still of that night the people of the city, most of whom had retired at their customary hour of nine o'clock, were wakened by the cries of the watchmen. Some in German, others in English, were shouting, their voices echoing among the buildings of the town: "Past twelve o'clock, and all is well — and Cornwallis has surrendered to General Washington!"

The rejoicing members of that Baptist convention passed this resolution:

"And now, dear Brethren, we feel ourselves constrained to acknowledge the great goodness of God toward us, and to call on you to join with us in thankfulness and praise, as well for the unanimity and brotherly love which prevailed throughout our meeting, as for the recent signal success granted to the American arms in the surrender of the whole British army under the command of Lord Cornwallis." [3]

Soon after victory was won, General Washington, Episcopal vestryman, wrote to the Baptist churches of Virginia through the officers of their state association: "I recollect with satisfaction that the religious society of which you are members have been throughout America, uniformly and almost unanimously, the firm friends to civil liberty and the persevering promoters of our glorious Revolution." [4]

At the beginning of the Revolutionary War, nine of the thirteen American colonies officially recognized and gave support to so-called "established" churches. Among the four New England states, only Rhode Island permitted complete freedom of worship—the legacy of Roger Williams and his Baptist followers. Congregationalism was the state religion of Connecticut, Massachusetts, and New Hampshire. The Episcopal Church was favored, in more or less degree, as established by law, in New York, Maryland, Virginia, North Carolina, South Carolina, and Georgia. New Jersey, Pennsylvania, and Delaware had no established religion.

Disestablishment came fairly early in the war for the southernmost states and for New York. In those states the influence of the Baptists, aided by Presbyterians and Methodists, the latter still part of the Episcopal Church although pulling steadily away, was the deciding factor for religious freedom. For the Baptists, the struggle was for complete separation of church and state, while Presbyterians and Methodists demanded only the safeguarding of their rights under acts of toleration.

In South Carolina the name of Richard Furman emerged as the man who led the forces against the established religion. In 1776 he sponsored a meeting at High Hills to discuss religious liberty and to lay plans to secure it in the Palmetto State. Two years later Furman visited the convention in Charleston that had met to draft a new state constitution, and his eloquent arguments resulted in the adoption of a provision that put an end to the special status of the Anglican Church in South Carolina and placed all churches on an equal footing of freedom.

The Episcopal Church in Virginia held out staunchly to preserve its established position. In the face of a flood of petitions from Baptists all over the Old Dominion, in December, 1779, the Assembly repealed parts of the act that had provided for the support of the clergy and for the collection and paying of parish levies. Another act of that Assembly provided that salaries for ministers would no longer be paid by the state.

These steps, restricting financial support for the Establishment, Baptists conceded, were in the right direction. But they were not enough to satisfy Baptist demands. The struggle in Virginia continued until after the war, when Thomas Jefferson's "Bill for the Establishment of Religious Freedom" brought victory for complete religious liberty in 1785. Not until 1817 did New Hampshire end its Congregational establishment. In 1818 Connecticut followed its neighbor's example.

A Wall of Separation

In Massachusetts, meanwhile, Backus continued his unrelenting war against levying taxes for the established church. The high point of his battle was reached in October, 1780, when he and his Baptist associates presented to the General Court of Massachusetts a vigorous protest against a provision in the proposed new state constitution which placed public education virtually under control of church leaders. The protest set forth specific reasons why Baptists opposed the plan, including these:

"Because it asserts a right in the people to give away a power they never had themselves; for no man has a right to judge for others in religious matters; yet this Article would give the majority of each town and parish the exclusive right of covenanting for the rest with religious teachers, and so of excluding the minority from the liberty of choosing for themselves in that respect.

"Because this power is given entirely into the hands of men who vote only by virtue of *money* qualifications, without any regard to the church of Christ.

"Because said Article contradicts itself; for it promises *equal* protection of all sects, with an exemption from any subordination of one religious denomination to another; when it is impossible for the majority of any community to govern in any affair, unless the minority are in subordination to them in that affair.

"Because by this Article the civil power is called to judge whether persons can conveniently and conscientiously attend upon any teacher within their reach, and oblige each one to support such teachers as may be contrary to his conscience; which is subversive of the unalienable rights of conscience." [5]

Elder Backus was elected a delegate to the Massachusetts convention called to ratify the proposed federal Constitution in 1787. The veteran crusader for religious freedom was gratified to know that the document, brought forth after long travail in Philadelphia, contained the words: "No religious test shall ever be required as a qualification to any office or public trust under the United States."

Still, Backus and his associates felt that this negative provision should be strengthened by a positive restraint upon the new government to prevent either public support, or interference in any manner, with religious affairs. They applauded James Madison's successful moves for the amendments, especially for the First Amendment, which erected what Thomas Jefferson later succinctly called the "wall of separation between church and state."

To the Baptists of the new American Republic the guarantees of the Bill of Rights were simply those for which they had fought and for which their forebears had suffered martyrdom in many areas of the world for centuries. They saw nothing remarkable about the provision that "Congress shall make no law respecting an establishment of religion, or prohibiting the free exercise thereof."

" 'Tis only the right of every person to believe or not to believe, and to be free of the meddling of the state in matters of conscience!" was the idea earnestly expressed by Baptist leaders and believers of that day.

Long after the adoption of the federal Constitution, Massachusetts retained its provision for recognition and support of the Congregational Church. "This is not just!" thundered Isaac Backus from his pulpit, as he spoke in the meetings of the Warren Baptist Association, and as he wrote letters of advice and encouragement to Baptists all over the state. In 1791 he issued a pamphlet calling attention to the conflict between the provision for religious liberty in the United States Constitution and that of the laws of his state, which clearly provided for an establishment of religion. He was answered by being reminded that the federal Constitution had no power to modify state constitutions and laws. Backus countered with the argument that the federal Constitution was by its own definition "the supreme law of the land," and that no state had the right to make and enforce laws that violated its provisions. In this fight Backus had the active support of such diverse fellowships as the Unitarians and the Quakers.

It was in 1833 that Massachusetts finally abandoned its provision for an established religion by a Bill of Rights in its constitution. Backus had planted among Baptists and others the seed of a political principle, deeply embedded in the rich soil of his religious faith, that in a Union of

States the rights of all citizens must be equally guaranteed. From that seed flowered the words of the Fourteenth Amendment to the United States Constitution:

"No state shall make or enforce any law which shall abridge the privileges and immunities of citizens of the United States, nor shall any state deprive any person of life, liberty, or property without due process of law, nor deny to any person within its jurisdiction the equal protection of the laws."

The Westward Tide of Settlers

Despite the hardships and hindrances of the War for Independence, Baptists continued their cooperation among neighboring congregations, and even across far distances, where communications and mutual assistance were still possible. In 1775 South Carolina Baptists raised funds to aid their brethren in New England who were being persecuted as nonconformists and nonsupporters of the established church.

Spurred by the realization that religious liberty had been secured through independence and the First Amendment in the Constitution, Baptists throughout the new Union moved forward in the establishment of congregations, forming associations, planning and carrying on missionary work among the Indians, and helping the struggling churches of the raw frontiers.

New Hampshire Baptists set up an association of churches in 1776, and helped to sponsor a similar group among Baptist churches of Maine. In 1781 the Shaftsbury Association brought together a number of Baptist churches in southern Vermont, western Massachusetts, and the eastern areas of New York state. In 1785 the Groton Conference was organized to serve many Baptist churches of Connecticut.

By 1795 there were enough Baptist churches in the vicinity of Otsego Lake, New York, to form an association. This organization proved to be a pioneer in what later became known as the Baptist Home Mission Society, for its member churches cooperated in raising funds to send the first missionary to preach to the Six Nations Indians of northern New York.

According to best available records kept by early Baptist historians, in 1790 there were in the United States 748 Baptist churches with about 60,970 members. These were served, somewhat inadequately, by 564 ordained preachers, their efforts supplemented by lay readers and so-called "exhorters." Ten years later, at the turn of the century, there were approximately 1250 Baptist churches in the expanding nation with total membership of about 100,000 souls. By 1810 the number of churches had grown to something more than 2000 with a total membership at that time of about 125,000.

Ever westward flowed the tide of settlers. With them went Baptist families in increasing numbers. Into the great northwestern states and territories they went, these immigrants principally from New England, New York, and Pennsylvania. They settled in the foothills of the Alleghenies, in the fertile farmlands and along the streams of the Ohio and the Mississippi valleys.

Especially attractive to Baptist immigrants was the Northwest Territory, lying north of the Ohio River, west of Pennsylvania and extending to the Mississippi River. An act of Congress known as the "Ordinance of 1787" guaranteed complete religious liberty and gave promise of free public schools in all that vast region. Article III of the Ordinance began with these words: "Religion, morality, and knowledge being necessary to good government and the happiness of mankind, schools and the means of education shall forever be encouraged."

In the area that became Ohio a band of twenty-five pioneers staked out their homesteads near the village of Columbia, now within the limits of Cincinnati. It was November 1788. Among them were two Baptists, Benjamin Stites, a Revolutionary major and recognized leader of the group, and John S. Gano, son of Dr. John Gano, the first Baptist pastor in New York City. In early 1790 came the Rev. Stephen Gano, another son of Pastor Gano. He helped the handful of Baptists who had settled at Columbia to organize a church, with Rev. John Smith as the first pastor.

Smith was a popular leader in public affairs in the pioneer community, an eloquent orator who became United States senator. Unfortunately, while in Washington he became associated with Aaron Burr and was involved in some of the schemes of this adventurer who barely missed defeating Thomas Jefferson for the presidency of the United States.

Cincinnati, with its land and water commerce, became the metropolis of the Northwest and also the center of Baptist activities and expansion. The Miami Association of Baptist Churches was organized in Cincinnati in June, 1798. The first Baptist church in Illinois was organized in 1796 at a village with the picturesque name of New Design. One family among the founders of this church produced six Baptist preachers—James Lemen and his five sons.

Baptists were the first Protestant denomination to carry the gospel and organize churches west of the Mississippi River. The first such congregation was formed in 1795 at a settlement in Missouri on the trail between the villages of St. Louis and St. Charles. It was called Fee Fee Baptist Church, and has had a continuous existence from its beginning.

By 1800 there were several Baptist congregations worshiping in homes or in small meeting houses in settlements
along the Mississippi and the Missouri rivers. In 1805 a group
of about twelve Baptists organized a church at the community of Tywappity, eleven miles south of the French town
of Cape Girardeau, Missouri. These earliest churches in the
Louisiana Territory drew worshipers by wagons or by horseback for miles around on meeting days—usually "oncet a
month."

Plentiful as Blackberries

A study completed in 1900 by Baptist historian J. M.
Carroll of Texas pictures the growth of the Baptists in the
southern states during the last decade of the eighteenth
century and the first ten or twelve years of the nineteenth.
In Virginia, where Dr. Carroll declared "Baptists were as
plentiful as blackberries," there were about 200 Baptist
churches with 20,000 members in 1790. One decade later
the numbers had grown to about 400 churches with 35,000
members.

Typical of the rugged pioneers who assembled the dissenters known as Baptists in humble homes or in groves of trees
and organized them into congregations was Elder Joshua
Morris. He preached in the numerous communities of the
state, and one June evening in 1780 he conducted a prayer
meeting in the home of John Franklin on Union Hill in
Richmond. Thirteen other persons of Baptist leanings were
present.

The house where the worshipers met for that service was
like most of the homes of the common people of that day
who became Baptists. It has been described as "a small
wooden building containing a single room of scarcely more
than sixteen or eighteen feet in dimensions, with a smaller

shed-room attached on the eastern side, and a chimney in the middle."

In that small shelter, despite the threat of invasion by the British forces moving northward from the Carolinas, the fourteen worshipers organized themselves into the First Baptist Church of Richmond. When some members of the small congregation urged caution in view of the possibility the town might be captured, Parson Morris is reported to have said: "Brethren! Let us take care of our souls, and the Lord—with the help of General Washington—will take care of the British!"

Brother Morris' faith proved well founded. The British never took Richmond, and the First Baptist Church of Richmond grew to be honored as a leading congregation of Virginia and the nation.

Baptists experienced similar leadership and expansion in the Carolinas. Their leader in that area in the post-Revolutionary period was Richard Furman, whose name is honored in a university founded by Baptists in Greenville, South Carolina. Furman grew up on a large cotton and tobacco plantation, son of wealthy parents who became ardent Whigs and supporters of the Revolution. Richard was ordained to preach and held revival services in numerous communities of his state.

When the War for Independence broke upon the Carolinas, Furman volunteered to join the troops. Governor John Rutledge persuaded him to remain a civilian and propagandize the American cause among the Tory-minded planters of western South Carolina. The eloquent young Furman spoke one evening at the settlement of Waxhaw, and in his audience were Widow Jackson and her two sons, John and Andrew Jackson. The British overran Waxhaw and a redcoat officer ordered Andrew to shine his boots. The

spirited lad refused, and the officer gave him a slash with
his sword that left a scar Andrew Jackson carried into the
President's mansion and to his grave. Furman performed
his task so well that the British general Lord Cornwallis
posted a reward of £1000 sterling for his capture. In later
years Furman became an outstanding leader in establishing
a true denomination from the scattered and independent
Baptist churches of America.

In Georgia the two great Baptist organizers of the pioneer
era were the Rev. Henry Holcombe, who in 1800 organized
the First Baptist Church of Savannah, and Dr. Jesse Mercer,
a preacher and educator who founded a college at Penfield,
that bears his name, and was later moved to Macon. Principally from Georgia and Tennessee, the settlers pushed
westward and southward into Alabama and Mississippi,
where they set up their cotton plantations with slave labor.

South of the Ohio River, into the territories that became
the states of Kentucky and Tennessee, the first settlers came
mostly from the mountainous areas of Virginia and North
Carolina. Then came the planters with their slaves, their
predominant ethnic background Scotch-Irish and their religion strongly Calvinist. While Presbyterians were most numerous among pioneers before the Revolution, Baptists out-
stripped them in the first decade of the nineteenth century.

Occasionally in the migrations to Kentucky and Tennessee
an entire congregation would decide to move at the same
time, including the preacher, deacons, and the members old
and young. They kept their worship going as they plodded
westward, holding their prayer meetings, singing their
hymns, and listening to the parson preach by the flickering
light of their camp fires.

Sunday Schools had their small beginnings near the turn
of the century and grew to exert a powerful influence in

the nationwide and worldwide Baptist fellowship. An example set in 1780 by a wealthy printer of Gloucester, England, was followed widely by Protestant churches in America. The printer was Robert Raikes, who, in a spirit of compassion for the dirty, ragged boys of the slums of his city, gathered several of them in his home on Sundays and gave them instruction in the Bible and the "three R's." A Baptist deacon, William Fox of England, expanded the movement in 1785 with an organization called "The Society for the Support and Encouragement of Sunday Schools." The first known Baptist Sunday School in the South devoted entirely to religious instruction was established in 1803 in the Second Baptist Church, Baltimore. In 1915, three women of the First Baptist Church of Philadelphia launched a Sunday School despite the protest of some leaders of their church who felt that the children would merely clutter up the house of worship.

Gradually, many Baptist ministers saw merit in the plan to teach religion to children meeting on Sunday in the churches and set up Bible classes. Often these preachers met the determined resistance of leaders of their congregations, who could find no scriptural basis for such goings on within the church walls. On the other hand, often the more liberal religious leaders decided that a Bible school for the young people was needed to instruct them in doctrine and morality. Thus, many Bible classes were established despite the opposition of the pastors.

One factor stimulating the founding of Sunday Schools in Baptist churches, as in the churches of other Protestant denominations, was the eagerness of children and youth, and for that matter of many adults, to hear something more than a steady diet of the dreary, long discourses delivered by most pastors to those early nineteenth-century congregations. The Sunday School brought Bible study down to the level of the immature and the uneducated, even when the minister himself was the only teacher.

The Frontier Communities

The fervor and intensity of the Great Awakening was never lost to the pioneer Baptist preachers and evangelists. "Seeking the lost" was their favorite theme. They preached it in their sermons and exhortations, in their Sunday services and in their "protracted meetings." They believed in a literal heaven and a literal hell, and they called men and women to repentance and faith in Jesus Christ with the principal aim to help the sinner to enjoy heaven and to avoid hell. As Dr. Nathan E. Wood expressed it in his discussion of the growth of Baptist theological thought:

"Preaching was azoic in its simplicity, literalness, and directness. Current philosophies appear to have had little influence on our preachers. French infidelity, whose brilliant reign in the United States during the last quarter of the Eighteenth and the first quarter of the Nineteenth centuries seems to have been a congenial sequel to the social and moral chaos incident to the Revolutionary War, was met by us not with intellectual subleties or argument, but by a rigid application of biblical truth to the consciences of men . . . Sneers at morality, jests at religion, and the whirl of worldly pleasure were met by a 'thus saith the Lord,' or the thunders of a prophesied judgment." [6]

Such was the dedication of the pioneer Baptist preachers and missionaries who went west with the settlers that they endured the hardships and risked all the dangers about them. Many brought with them their brides of a few days or their wives of many years, who shared with their husbands the rugged life and work in the wilderness communities of the immigrants. They had faith in God and they were convinced that out on the frontier were people who needed the old-time religion. They had a message and they aimed to tell it. Their aim struck the hearts of the pioneer people, a people hungry for something that would bring hope and faith into their drab lives, something to lighten their loads of toil and to brighten the dismal boredom of the perpetual fight for existence against nature and the elements.

At the beginning of the nineteenth century most Baptist meeting houses in the cities and towns of the eastern states had progressed to neat structures of brick or white-painted wood. They usually had a bay window extension which partially surrounded the pulpit where the minister delivered his sermons. Many were heated by Franklin stoves, considered adequate since cold-natured members could move nearer for greater comfort.

The typical church building of the pioneer Baptist congregation, however, was a rude log structure about twenty by thirty feet, often with split-log benches with or without backs. A stick-and-mud fireplace when packed with seasoned logs provided heat during the cold season, and open windows permitted cooling breezes when the sun bore down. The meeting houses were usually built by volunteer labor of the men and boys of the congregations with only a boss carpenter to supervise the work. Women and girls of the families supplied and served the noon meal.

A center aisle in the meeting house divided the congregation so that the male worshipers sat on one side and the females on the other. Singers might be seated on benches to the right or left of the raised pulpit platform, but never with men and women on the same benches. In front and at the sides of the meeting house were hitching posts for the horses that brought in the worshipers, sometimes from as far as twenty miles away.

The Preacher Got a Dollar a Day

The preacher was "called" by the congregation, whose members decided his tenure and pay. He rode his own horse and brought his own Bible in his saddlebags—along with his nightshirt and little else. It was his due to be entertained by the members of the church, although it usually meant that he slept with one or more of the boys of the host family. Once-a-month preaching services allowed him to hold as many as four pastorates at one time, although many were content with two. His pay was generally one dollar per meeting day—considered a fair wage and in keeping with the scale for a skilled worker. Many pioneer preachers, the most educated men of their communities, set up subscription schools to teach the children of their members to read and write, and to add to their meager incomes.

The frontier Baptist churches had no budgets, no finance committees, no literature to buy, practically no expenses and, therefore, no worry about them. If the church building needed repairs or paint, the men of the congregation supplied the need. Fuel could be had for gathering it in the clearing. Families took turns sweeping out the meeting house and keeping its grounds neat.

A cemetery was as much a part of the pioneer place of worship as the building itself. The burial place filled slowly with the mortal remains of the families within the fellowship—the aged, the infants and children who could not survive the rigors of frontier life, those in their prime who died from mysterious diseases supposed to be incurable—all those snatched away by the Grim Reaper. The cemetery became a tie that bound the worshipers all the closer in memories of the joys and sorrows of the departed ones.

Discipline was severely enforced in the pioneer Baptist churches. Hardly a scheduled business meeting convened but what some hapless member was mentioned by the elders as needing spiritual chastisement. It might be a deacon seen taking a hospitable dram, or a young man who, rumor had it, went to a square dance at an unbeliever's home and thus got into bad company. From the minutes of the Forks of the Elkhorn Baptist Church in Kentucky, compiled from 1800 to 1820, Dr. Archie Robertson has gleaned these items in his work *That Old-Time Religion:*

"Bro. Blanton complains against Bro. Major for playing carnal plays. Bro. Edward Roberts is excluded from this church for playing fives and for offering to bet One Hundred Dollars. Mr. Asa Bolls Caty is Excluded for the sin of a Dultery. Sister Esther Boulware's Winney (a slave) was given a hearing on charges that since the Lord converted her, 'She had never believed that any Christians kept Negroes a slave, and that she believed There was thousands of White people wallowing in Hell for their treatment of Negroes and she did not care if there was as many more.' Winnie was excluded from that church." [7]

Never did the Baptist pioneer preachers and church leaders lose sight of the principle of freedom in church control, with each congregation, however few in numbers or humble in the social standing of its members, autonomous and free to select its pastor, ordain its deacons, admit new members, administer its discipline, care for its religious teaching and training, and cooperate with other congregations as its members might decide.

And never did they forget that freedom of conscience and worship was their cherished right, to be fought for without retreat or compromise.

AND FINALLY . . .

From the Past to the Future

American Christians owe everlasting thanks to the God
of all nations, for the men and women of more than two
centuries ago who caught the vision of freedom of conscience
and of worship. Against all opposition, both in established
churches and legislative bodies, they fought for their belief
in liberty.

From that fundamental freedom, the American people
have enjoyed all other human liberties for these two hundred
years: Freedom of speech, of the press, of peaceful assembly;
the right of every person to petition the government; to
be considered innocent until proved guilty in a fair trial;
and all other guarantees of freedom permanently embedded
in our Constitution and its Bill of Rights.

One of the famous patriots of 200 years ago, Patrick
Henry of Virginia, who staunchly defended freedom of religion, declared: "I have but one lamp by which my feet
are guided, and that is the lamp of experience. I know no
way of judging the future but by the past."

Will those liberties be enjoyed 200 years from now, by
the children of the present generations? Will there be no
breakdown of what Thomas Jefferson, author of the Declara-

tion of Independence, so aptly called "a wall of separation of church and state?" Will there be no heavy hand of censorship upon peaceful communications, no restrictions upon ideas and the search for truth, no hindrance to its expression by any and all media?

We fervently hope and pray that "indomitable Baptists" of this era will be responsible Christian citizens and, in gratitude for the heritage of liberty they enjoy in this country, use their power to help shape the world for peace and freedom under God.

The Armstrongs

November 28, 1974

NOTES

Chapter One

1. Joseph Martin Dawson, *Baptists and the American Republic* (Nashville: Broadman Press, 1956).

2. *Ibid.*, p. 91.

3. William Cabell Rives, *History of the Life and Times of James Madison* (Boston: Little, Brown & Co.).

4. L. H. Butterfield, *Elder John Leland, Jeffersonian Itinerant* (Worcester, Mass.: American Antiquarian Society).

5. Saul K. Padover, ed., *The Complete Jefferson* (New York: Duell, Sloan & Pearce).

6. Robert B. Semple, *History of the Rise and Progress of the Baptists in Virginia* (Richmond: Robert B. Semple, 1810).

7. *Ibid.*

8. Butterfield, *op. cit.*

9. Dawson, *op. cit.*

10. Irving Brant, *Father of the Constitution* (Indianapolis, Ind.: Bobbs-Merrill Co.).

Chapter Two

1. Henry Martyn Dexter, *Roger Williams* (Philadelphia: American Baptist Publication Society, 1876).

2. Isaac Backus, *Church History of New England* (Philadelphia: American Baptist Publication Society, 1844).

3. *Ibid.*

4. *Ibid.*

Chapter Three
1. Backus, *op. cit.*
2. *Ibid.*
3. *Ibid.*
4. Dawson, *op. cit.*
5. *Ibid.*
6. Backus, *op. cit.*
7. *Ibid.*

Chapter Four
1. William L. Lumpkin, *Baptist Foundations in the South* (Nashville: Broadman Press, 1961).
2. Morgan Edwards' manuscript is in the library of Furman University, Greenville, South Carolina.
3. Joe M. King, *A History of South Carolina Baptists* (Columbia, S.C.: The General Board of the South Carolina Baptist Convention, 1964).

Chapter Five
1. The account of James Lane of Virginia is from the manuscript by Morgan Edwards, *op. cit.*
2. *Ibid.*
3. T. B. Maston, *Isaac Backus—Pioneer of Religious Liberty,* doctoral thesis (Yale University Press, 1939).
4. *Ibid.*
5. Isaac Backus, *A History of New England, with Particular Reference to the Denomination of Christians Called Baptists,* Vol. II. (Providence, R.I.: privately published, 1784).
6. Quoted by Backus from copy of original bearing signature of John Hancock.

Chapter Six
1. Maston, *op. cit.*
2. Backus, *op. cit.*
3. Quoted in various sources from the original minutes preserved by the American Baptist Convention, Valley Forge, Pennsylvania.
4. Backus, *op. cit.*
5. Alvah Hovey, *Memoir of the Life and Times of the Rev. Isaac Backus,* (Philadelphia: American Baptist Publication Society, 1898).

6. A. H. Newman, ed., *A Century of Baptist Achievement* (Philadelphia: American Baptist Publication Society, 1901).

7. Archie Robertson, *That Old-Time Religion* (Boston: Houghton Mifflin Co., 1950).